PRACTICE SOCCER
BY YOURSELF

To Diane and the Vienna Panthers for inspiration. To Donna and the Vienna Raiders for perspiration.

PRACTICE SOCCER BY YOURSELF

Ken Mallory

Illustrations: A. J. Hoehn

ICARUS PRESS
South Bend, Indiana
1984

PRACTICE SOCCER BY YOURSELF
Copyright (c) 1984 by Ken Mallory

All rights reserved. No part of this book may be used or reproduced in any manner whatsoever without the written permission of the publisher, except in the case of brief quotations embodied in critical articles or reviews.

Manufactured in the United States of America.

1 2 3 4 5 6 87 86 85 84

Icarus Press, Inc.
P.O. Box 1225
South Bend, IN 46624

Library of Congress Cataloging in Publication Data
Mallory, Ken, 1940-
    Practice Soccer by Yourself.

    1. Soccer--Training--Juvenile literature.
I. Hoehn, A.J. II. Title.
GV943.9.T7M3 1984   796.334'2   84-15854
ISBN 0-89651-606-7 (pbk.)

TABLE OF CONTENTS

PRACTICE SOCCER BY YOURSELF

How To Use This Book

The drills in this book will help you learn how to play soccer well. You can do all of the drills by yourself. Follow the instructions and you will learn quickly and see yourself improve.

There are six parts to this book:

1. Volley Kicking
2. Shooting
3. Juggling
4. Dribbling
5. Stopping the ball
6. Rebounding

There are twenty drills in each part. The first drill in each is the easiest to do. The second is a little harder than the first, and the third is a little harder than the second. So you should be sure to start with the first drill and work your way up.

When you practice, try to do six drills every day — one from each part of the book. Be sure to keep score on each drill. This will help you see your progress.

Remember — if you don't understand something, ask your coach or parents to explain it.

If you know a good drill that you think should be in this book, please write it down on page **261** and mail it in. If it is used in the next edition you will receive a $100.00 prize.

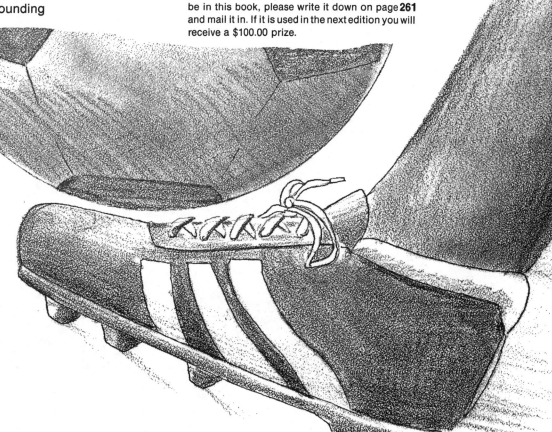

Dear Parent,

This book has been written to help your child improve his or her basic soccer skills. The six sections of the book contain practice drills that need very little equipment, preparation and time.

The drills in each section progress from easy to difficult. So as your child grows in skill and confidence, new and more challenging skills can be practiced.

Each drill lists the equipment that is needed and describes how to set up and conduct the drill. Also each provides a chart to record progress. If your child follows the recommended daily program of practicing one drill from each of the six sections, daily practices will take about 30 minutes.

Drills have been illustrated to help children understand them; however, younger children may need some help.

If you would like to recommend improvements to the book, please send your comments to:

PRACTICE SOCCER BY YOURSELF
c/o H.D. Jones
Florance Gordon and Brown
815 Mutual Bldg.
Richmond, VA 23219

I hope that soccer will be a healthy and happy experience for your child.

Sincerely.

Ken Mallory

A Note For Coaches

The intent of this book is to give young soccer players a set of skill development drills that can be practiced alone, with very little equipment, setup and time required.

There are six major parts to this book:

1. Volley Kicking
2. Shooting
3. Juggling
4. Dribbling
5. Stopping the ball
6. Rebounding

The drills in each section progress from easy to difficult. All the young players needs to do is start at the beginning and as he or she masters on drill, move on to the next.

Detailed instructions on how to set up, conduct, and keep score are given with each drill. At the end of the book is a checklist where a player can chart his or her overall progress.

Many coaches already prescribe homework drills for their players. If you have some favorite drill missing from this book that you would like to see included, please send us a description. A form is given on page 261, please mail it to:

PRACTICE SOCCER BY YOURSELF
c/o H.D. Jones
Florance Gordon and Brown
815 Mutual Bldg.
Richmond, VA 23219

If your drill is chosen for the next edition, you and your club (if you wish) will be credited and you will receive a $100.00 prize.

Why Should You Practice. . .

. . .VOLLEY KICKING

Picture yourself in the last few minutes of a soccer game. The score is tied 1 to 1. Your team is attacking the other team's goal.

Your right wing kicks the ball in the air towards you. Now, think about what you might do. If you can kick the ball quickly, you have a good shot on the goal. If you can't shoot quickly, the other team's defenders will move between you and the goal and keep you from shooting.

Of course, you have been practicing your volley kicks. As the ball drops in front of you, you kick it before it hits the ground (this is called a volley kick). The goalie goes down for the ball — too late. Your team wins 2 to 1.

When the ball is coming to you in the air (as often it does) stopping it and bringing it under control takes time. If you take too long to control the it, players from the other team can block shots or passes or take the ball away.

You don't always have to volleykick, but when players from the other team are close by, volley kicks make good shots, clearing kicks and passes.

The following drills will help you learn to do two types of volley kicks:

1. **FULL VOLLEY** — When you kick the ball before it touches the ground.

2. **HALF VOLLEY** — When you kick the ball immediately after it touches the ground.

FULL VOLLEY

What You Need To Do This Drill

- A small area of flat ground with a wall at one end
- A soccer ball
- A piece of chalk
- 2 markers (rags, sticks, cans, boxes, cones, etc.)
- This page, a pencil and an eraser

How To Set Up For This Drill

A. Place 2 markers 6 steps away from the wall. When you kick the ball you must be farther from the wall than the markers are.

MARKER 6 STEPS FROM WALL

MARKER 6 STEPS FROM WALL

How To Do This Drill

1. Stand facing the wall. Stand further from the wall than the markers.

2. Throw the ball straight up a little over your head.

3. Before the ball hits the ground, kick the ball at the wall.

4. Give yourself **1 point** if you kicked the ball before it bounced. Give yourself **1 more point** if the ball hit the wall. Write down your points in **"Today's Scores."**

5. Do this drill 20 times.

6. After you have done the drill 20 times, add up your points. This is your score.

NOTE: Look at the ball as you kick it.

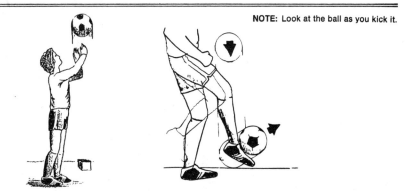

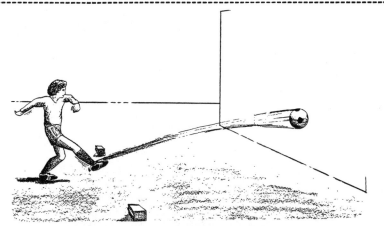

YOUR GOAL: A score of 15 or more points

Today's Scores

	1	2	3	4	5	6	7	8	9	10	11	12	13	14	15	16	17	18	19	20	TOTAL
KICKS																					
HIT THE WALL																						

How To Watch Your Score Improve

1. Write down your score for today. The first day you do this drill, write your score by **DAY 1**, Write you score for the second day by **DAY 2**, and so on.

2. Did you meet your goal?

NO!

Erase **"Today's Scores"** and do this drill again the next time you **PRACTICE SOCCER BY YOURSELF.**

YES!

WELL DONE! The next time you **PRACTICE SOCCER BY YOURSELF** you can move up to the drill on the next page.

Also cut off the number on the top of this page. Then turn to the **PROGRESS CHART** at the end of the book.

DAY	SCORE	DAY	SCORE	DAY	SCORE
1		11		21	
2		12		22	
3		13		23	
4		14		24	
5		15		25	
6		16		26	
7		17		27	
8		18		28	
9		19		29	
10		20		30	

NOTES:

FULL VOLLEY WITH THE WEAKER FOOT

What You Need To Do This Drill
- A small area of flat ground with a wall at one end
- A soccer ball
- A piece of chalk
- 2 markers (rags, sticks, cans, boxes, cones, etc.)
- This page, a pencil and an eraser

How To Set Up For This Drill
A. Place 2 markers 6 steps away from the wall. When you kick the ball you must be farther from the wall than the markers are.

MARKER 6 STEPS FROM WALL

MARKER 6 STEPS FROM WALL

How To Do This Drill

1. Stand facing the wall. Stand further from the wall than the markers.

2. Throw the ball straight up a little over your head.

3. Before the ball hits the ground, kick the ball at the wall with your weaker foot.

4. Give yourself **1 point** if you kicked the ball before it bounced. Give yourself **1 more point** if the ball hit the wall. Write down your points in **"Today's Scores"**.

5. Do this drill 20 times.

6. After you have done the drill 20 times, add up your points. This is your score.

NOTE: Look at the ball as you kick it.

NOTE: Your weaker foot is the one you don't usually use to kick the ball. If you are right handed your left foot is likely to be your weaker foot. If you are left handed your right foot is likely to be your weaker.

YOUR GOAL: A score of 10 or more points

Today's Scores

	1	2	3	4	5	6	7	8	9	10	11	12	13	14	15	16	17	18	19	20	TOTAL
KICKS																					
HIT THE WALL																					

How To Watch Your Score Improve

1. Write down your score for today. The first day you do this drill, write your score by **DAY 1**, Write you score for the second day by **DAY 2**, and so on.

2. Did you meet your goal?

NO!

Erase **"Today's Scores"** and do this drill again the next time you **PRACTICE SOCCER BY YOURSELF.**

YES!

WELL DONE! The next time you **PRACTICE SOCCER BY YOURSELF** you can move up to the drill on the next page.

Also cut off the number on the top of this page. Then turn to the **PROGRESS CHART** at the end of the book.

DAY	SCORE	DAY	SCORE	DAY	SCORE
1		11		21	
2		12		22	
3		13		23	
4		14		24	
5		15		25	
6		16		26	
7		17		27	
8		18		28	
9		19		29	
10		20		30	

NOTES:

PASSING FULL VOLLEY

What You Need To Do This Drill

- A small area of flat ground with a wall at one end
- A soccer ball
- A piece of chalk
- 2 markers (rags, sticks, cans, boxes, cones, etc.)
- This page, a pencil and an eraser

How To Set Up For This Drill

A. Place 2 markers 6 steps away from the wall. When you kick the ball you must be farther from the wall than the markers are.

B. Draw a line on the wall 6 large steps long and as high as your waist. You must kick the ball under the line.

6 STEPS

MARKER 6 STEPS FROM WALL

MARKER 6 STEPS FROM WALL

How To Do This Drill

1. Stand facing the wall. Stand further from the wall than the markers.

2. Throw the ball straight up a little over your head.

3. Before the ball hits the ground, kick the ball at the wall with the inside of either foot. Kick the ball under the line.

4. Give yourself **1 point** if you kicked the ball before it bounced. Give yourself **1 more point** if the ball hit the wall under the line. Write down your points in **"Today's Scores."**

5. Do this drill 20 times.

6. After you have done the drill 20 times, add up your points. This is your score.

NOTE: Look at the ball as you kick it.

NOTE: To kick the ball low, bend your body forward over the ball.

NOTE: To kick the ball low, kick it at or above its center point.

YOUR GOAL: A score of 20 or more points

Today's Scores

	1	2	3	4	5	6	7	8	9	10	11	12	13	14	15	16	17	18	19	20	TOTAL
KICKS																					
HIT THE WALL																					

How To Watch Your Score Improve

1. Write down your score for today. The first day you do this drill, write your score by **DAY 1**, Write you score for the second day by **DAY 2**, and so on.

2. Did you meet your goal?

NO!

Erase **"Today's Scores"** and do this drill again the next time you **PRACTICE SOCCER BY YOURSELF.**

YES!

WELL DONE! The next time you **PRACTICE SOCCER BY YOURSELF** you can move up to the drill on the next page.

Also cut off the number on the top of this page. Then turn to the **PROGRESS CHART** at the end of the book.

DAY	SCORE	DAY	SCORE	DAY	SCORE
1		11		21	
2		12		22	
3		13		23	
4		14		24	
5		15		25	
6		16		26	
7		17		27	
8		18		28	
9		19		29	
10		20		30	

NOTES:

PASSING FULL VOLLEY WITH THE WEAKER FOOT

What You Need To Do This Drill

- A small area of flat ground with a wall at one end
- A soccer ball
- A piece of chalk
- 2 markers (rags, sticks, cans, boxes, cones, etc.)
- This page, a pencil and an eraser

How To Set Up For This Drill

A. Place 2 markers 6 steps away from the wall. When you kick the ball you must be farther from the wall than the markers are.

B. Draw a line on the wall 6 large steps long and as high as your waist. You must kick the ball under this line.

6 STEPS

MARKER 6 STEPS FROM WALL

MARKER 6 STEPS FROM WALL

How To Do This Drill

1. Stand facing the wall. Stand further from the wall than the markers.

2. Throw the ball straight up a little over your head.

3. Before the ball hits the ground, kick the ball with the inside of your weaker foot. Kick the ball under the line

4. Give yourself **1 point** if you kicked the ball before it bounced. Give yourself **1 more point** if the ball hit the wall under the line. Write down your points in **"Today's Scores."**

5. Do this drill 20 times.

6. After you have done the drill 20 times, add up your points. This is your score.

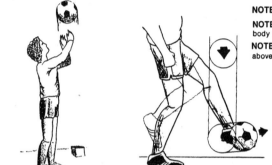

NOTE. Look at the ball as you kick it.

NOTE: To kick the ball low, bend your body forward over the ball.

NOTE: To kick the ball low, kick it at or above its center point.

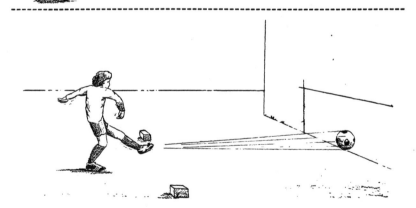

YOUR GOAL: A score of 15 or more points

Today's Scores

	1	2	3	4	5	6	7	8	9	10	11	12	13	14	15	16	17	18	19	20	YOUR SCORE
KICKS																					
HIT THE WALL																					

How To Watch Your Score Improve

1. Write down your score for today. The first day you do this drill, write your score by **DAY 1**, Write you score for the second day by **DAY 2**, and so on.

2. Did you meet your goal?

NO!

Erase **"Today's Scores"** and do this drill again the next time you **PRACTICE SOCCER BY YOURSELF.**

YES!

WELL DONE! The next time you **PRACTICE SOCCER BY YOURSELF** you can move up to the drill on the next page.

Also cut off the number on the top of this page. Then turn to the **PROGRESS CHART** at the end of the book.

DAY	SCORE	DAY	SCORE	DAY	SCORE
1		11		21	
2		12		22	
3		13		23	
4		14		24	
5		15		25	
6		16		26	
7		17		27	
8		18		28	
9		19		29	
10		20		30	

NOTES:

CLEARING FULL VOLLEY

What You Need To Do This Drill

- A small area of flat ground with a wall at one end
- A soccer ball
- A piece of chalk
- 2 markers (rags, sticks, cans, boxes, cones, etc.)
- This page, a pencil and an eraser

How To Set Up For This Drill

A. Place 2 markers 6 steps away from the wall. When you kick the ball you must be farther from the wall than the markers are.

B. Draw a line on the wall 6 large steps long and as high as the top of your head. You must kick the ball over this line.

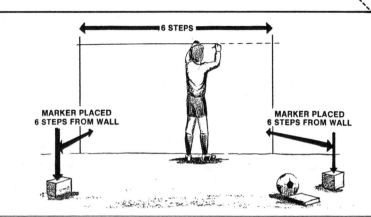

How To Do This Drill

1. Stand facing the wall. Stand further from the wall than the markers.

2. Throw the ball straight up a little over your head.

3. Before the ball hits the ground, kick the ball at the wall with the top (instep) of either foot. Kick the ball over the line.

4. Give yourself **1 point** if you kicked the ball before it bounced. Give yourself **1 more point** if the ball hit the wall over the line. Write down your points in **"Today's Scores."**

5. Do this drill 20 times.

6. After you have done the drill 20 times, add up your points. This is your score.

NOTE: Look at the ball as you kick it.
NOTE: To kick the ball high, bend your body backward away from the ball.
NOTE: To kick the ball high, kick it below its center point.

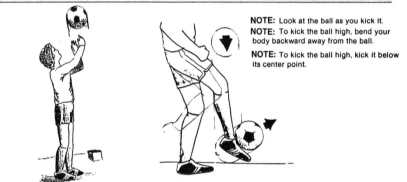

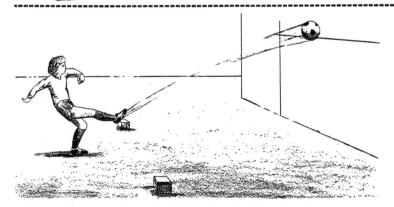

YOUR GOAL: A score of 20 or more points

Today's Scores

	1	2	3	4	5	6	7	8	9	10	11	12	13	14	15	16	17	18	19	20	TOTAL
KICKS																					
HIT THE WALL																					

How To Watch Your Score Improve

1. Write down your score for today. The first day you do this drill, write your score by **DAY 1,** Write you score for the second day by **DAY 2,** and so on.

2. Did you meet your goal?

NO!

Erase **"Today's Scores"** and do this drill again the next time you **PRACTICE SOCCER BY YOURSELF.**

YES!

WELL DONE! The next time you **PRACTICE SOCCER BY YOURSELF** you can move up to the drill on the next page.

Also cut off the number on the top of this page. Then turn to the **PROGRESS CHART** at the end of the book.

DAY	SCORE	DAY	SCORE	DAY	SCORE
1		11		21	
2		12		22	
3		13		23	
4		14		24	
5		15		25	
6		16		26	
7		17		27	
8		18		28	
9		19		29	
10		20		30	

NOTES:

CLEARING FULL VOLLEY WITH THE WEAKER FOOT

What You Need To Do This Drill

- A small area of flat ground with a wall at one end
- A soccer ball
- A piece of chalk
- 2 markers (rags, sticks, cans, boxes, cones, etc.)
- This page, a pencil and an eraser

How To Set Up For This Drill

A. Place 2 markers 6 steps away from the wall. When you kick the ball you must be farther from the wall than the markers are.

B. Draw a line on the wall 6 large steps long and as high as the top of your head. You must kick the ball over this line.

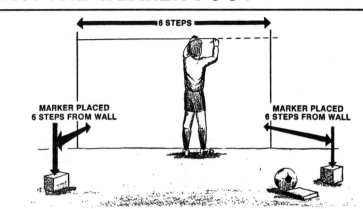

6 STEPS

MARKER PLACED 6 STEPS FROM WALL

MARKER PLACED 6 STEPS FROM WALL

How To Do This Drill

1. Stand facing the wall. Stand further from the wall than the markers.

2. Throw the ball straight up a little over your head.

3. Before the ball hits the ground, kick the ball at the wall with the top (instep) your weaker foot. Kick the ball over the line.

4. Give yourself **1 point** if you kicked the ball before it bounced. Give yourself **1 more point** if the ball hit the wall over the line. Write down your points in **"Today's Scores."**

5. Do this drill 20 times.

6. After you have done the drill 20 times, add up your points. This is your score.

NOTE: Look at the ball as you kick it.

NOTE: Your weaker foot is the one you don't usually use to kick the ball. If you are right handed your left foot is likely to be your weaker foot. If you are left handed your right foot is likely to be your weaker.

NOTE: To kick the ball high, bend your body backward away from the ball.

NOTE: To kick the ball high, kick it below its center point.

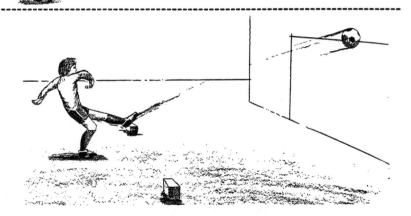

YOUR GOAL: A score of 15 or more points

Today's Scores

	1	2	3	4	5	6	7	8	9	10	11	12	13	14	15	16	17	18	19	20	TOTAL
KICKS																					
HIT THE WALL																					

How To Watch Your Score Improve

1. Write down your score for today. The first day you do this drill, write your score by **DAY 1**, Write you score for the second day by **DAY 2**, and so on.

2. Did you meet your goal?

NO!

Erase **"Today's Scores"** and do this drill again the next time you **PRACTICE SOCCER BY YOURSELF**.

YES!

WELL DONE! The next time you **PRACTICE SOCCER BY YOURSELF** you can move up to the drill on the next page.

Also cut off the number on the top of this page. Then turn to the **PROGRESS CHART** at the end of the book.

DAY	SCORE	DAY	SCORE	DAY	SCORE
1		11		21	
2		12		22	
3		13		23	
4		14		24	
5		15		25	
6		16		26	
7		17		27	
8		18		28	
9		19		29	
10		20		30	

NOTES:

PASSING FULL VOLLEY

What You Need To Do This Drill

- A small area of flat ground with a wall at one end
- A soccer ball
- A piece of chalk
- 2 markers (rags, sticks, cans, boxes, cones, etc.)
- This page, a pencil and an eraser

How To Set Up For This Drill

A. Place 2 markers 6 steps away from the wall. When you kick the ball you must be farther from the wall than the markers are.

B. Draw a line on the wall 6 large steps long and as high as your waist. You must kick the ball under the line.

6 STEPS

MARKER 6 STEPS FROM WALL

MARKER 6 STEPS FROM WALL

How To Do This Drill

1. Stand facing the wall. Stand further from the wall than the markers.

2. Throw the ball straight up a few feet over your head.

3. Before the ball hits the ground, kick the ball at the wall with the inside of either foot. Kick the ball under the line.

4. Give yourself **1 point** if you kicked the ball before it bounced. Give yourself **1 more point** if the ball hit the wall under the line. Write down your points in **"Today's Scores."**

5. Do this drill 20 times.

6. After you have done the drill 20 times, add up your points. This is your score.

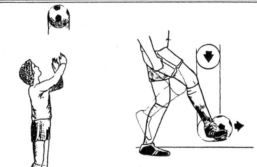

NOTE: Look at the ball as you kick it.

NOTE: To kick the ball low, bend your body forward over the ball.

NOTE: To kick the ball low, kick it at or above its center point.

YOUR GOAL: A score of 30 or more points

Today's Scores

	1	2	3	4	5	6	7	8	9	10	11	12	13	14	15	16	17	18	19	20	TOTAL
KICKS																					
HIT THE WALL																						

How To Watch Your Score Improve

1. Write down your score for today. The first day you do this drill, write your score by **DAY 1**, Write you score for the second day by **DAY 2**, and so on.

2. Did you meet your goal?

NO!

Erase **"Today's Scores"** and do this drill again the next time you **PRACTICE SOCCER BY YOURSELF.**

YES!

WELL DONE! The next time you **PRACTICE SOCCER BY YOURSELF** you can move up to the drill on the next page.

Also cut off the number on the top of this page. Then turn to the **PROGRESS CHART** at the end of the book.

DAY	SCORE
1	
2	
3	
4	
5	
6	
7	
8	
9	
10	

DAY	SCORE
11	
12	
13	
14	
15	
16	
17	
18	
19	
20	

DAY	SCORE
21	
22	
23	
24	
25	
26	
27	
28	
29	
30	

NOTES:

PASSING FULL VOLLEY WITH THE WEAKER FOOT

What You Need To Do This Drill

- A small area of flat ground with a wall at one end
- A soccer ball
- A piece of chalk
- 2 markers (rags, sticks, cans, boxes, cones, etc.)
- This page, a pencil and an eraser

How To Set Up For This Drill

A. Place 2 markers 6 steps away from the wall. When you kick the ball you must be farther from the wall than the markers are.

B. Draw a line on the wall 6 large steps long and as high as your waist. You must kick the ball under this line.

6 STEPS

MARKER 6 STEPS FROM WALL

MARKER 6 STEPS FROM WALL

How To Do This Drill

1. Stand facing the wall. Stand further from the wall than the markers.

2. Throw the ball straight up a few feet over your head.

3. Before the ball hits the ground, kick the ball with the inside of your weaker foot. Kick the ball under the line

4. Give yourself **1 point** if you kicked the ball before it bounced. Give yourself **1 more point** if the ball hit the wall under the line. Write down your points in **"Today's Scores."**

5. Do this drill 20 times.

6. After you have done the drill 20 times, add up your points. This is your score.

NOTE: Look at the ball as you kick it.

NOTE: To kick the ball low, bend your body forward over the ball.

NOTE: To kick the ball low, kick it at or above its center point.

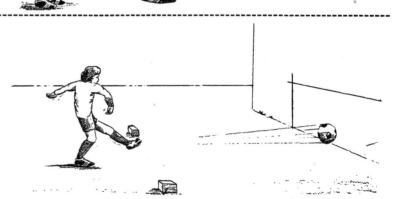

YOUR GOAL: A score of 20 or more points

Today's Scores

	1	2	3	4	5	6	7	8	9	10	11	12	13	14	15	16	17	18	19	20	TOTAL
KICKS																					
HIT THE WALL																					

How To Watch Your Score Improve

1. Write down your score for today. The first day you do this drill, write your score by **DAY 1**, Write you score for the second day by **DAY 2**, and so on.

2. Did you meet your goal?

NO!

Erase **"Today's Scores"** and do this drill again the next time you **PRACTICE SOCCER BY YOURSELF.**

YES!

WELL DONE! The next time you **PRACTICE SOCCER BY YOURSELF** you can move up to the drill on the next page.

Also cut off the number on the top of this page. Then turn to the **PROGRESS CHART** at the end of the book.

DAY	SCORE
1	
2	
3	
4	
5	
6	
7	
8	
9	
10	

DAY	SCORE
11	
12	
13	
14	
15	
16	
17	
18	
19	
20	

DAY	SCORE
21	
22	
23	
24	
25	
26	
27.	
28	
29	
30	

NOTES:

HALF VOLLEY

What You Need To Do This Drill
- A small area of flat ground with a wall at one end
- A soccer ball
- A piece of chalk
- 2 markers (rags, sticks, cans, boxes, cones, etc.)
- This page, a pencil and an eraser

How To Set Up For This Drill
A. Place 2 markers 6 steps away from the wall. When you kick the ball you must be farther from the wall than the markers are.

MARKER 6 STEPS FROM WALL

MARKER 6 STEPS FROM WALL

How To Do This Drill
1. Stand facing the wall. Stand further from the wall than the markers.

2. Throw the ball straight up a little over your head.

3. Immediately after the ball hits the ground, kick the ball at the wall with either foot.

4. Give yourself **1 point** if you kicked the ball immediately after it bounced. Give yourself **1 more point** if the ball hit the wall. Write down your points in **"Today's Scores."**

5. Do this drill 20 times.

6. After you have done the drill 20 times, add up your points. This is your score.

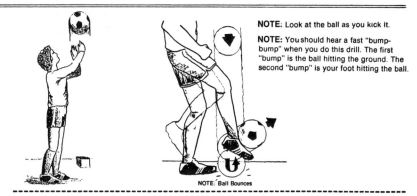

NOTE: Look at the ball as you kick it.

NOTE: You should hear a fast "bump-bump" when you do this drill. The first "bump" is the ball hitting the ground. The second "bump" is your foot hitting the ball.

NOTE: Ball Bounces

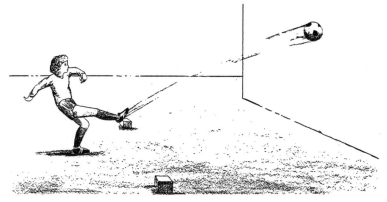

YOUR GOAL: A score of 15 or more points

Today's Scores

	1	2	3	4	5	6	7	8	9	10	11	12	13	14	15	16	17	18	19	20	TOTAL
KICKS																					
HIT THE WALL																					

How To Watch Your Score Improve

1. Write down your score for today. The first day you do this drill, write your score by **DAY 1**, Write you score for the second day by **DAY 2**, and so on.

2. Did you meet your goal?

NO!

Erase **"Today's Scores"** and do this drill again the next time you **PRACTICE SOCCER BY YOURSELF.**

YES!

WELL DONE! The next time you **PRACTICE SOCCER BY YOURSELF** you can move up to the drill on the next page.

Also cut off the number on the top of this page. Then turn to the **PROGRESS CHART** at the end of the book.

DAY	SCORE	DAY	SCORE	DAY	SCORE
1		11		21	
2		12		22	
3		13		23	
4		14		24	
5		15		25	
6		16		26	
7		17		27	
8		18		28	
9		19		29	
10		20		30	

NOTES:

HALF VOLLEY WITH THE WEAKER FOOT

What You Need To Do This Drill
- A small area of flat ground with a wall at one end
- A soccer ball
- A piece of chalk
- 2 markers (rags, sticks, cans, boxes, cones, etc.)
- This page, a pencil and an eraser

How To Set Up For This Drill
A. Place 2 markers 6 steps away from the wall. When you kick the ball you must be farther from the wall than the markers are.

MARKER 6 STEPS FROM WALL

MARKER 6 STEPS FROM WALL

How To Do This Drill

1. Stand facing the wall. Stand further from the wall than the markers.

2. Throw the ball straight up a little over your head.

3. Immediately after the ball hits the ground, kick the ball at the wall with your weaker foot.

4. Give yourself **1 point** if you kicked the ball immediately after it bounced. Give yourself **1 more point** if the ball hit the wall. Write down your points in **"Today's Scores."**

5. Do this drill 20 times.

6. After you have done the drill 20 times, add up your points. This is your score.

NOTE: Ball Bounces

NOTE: Look at the ball as you kick it.

NOTE: Your weaker foot is the one you don't usually use to kick the ball. If you are right handed your left foot is likely to be your weaker foot. If you are left handed your right foot is likely to be your weaker.

NOTE: You should hear a fast "bump-bump" when you do this drill. The first "bump" is the ball hitting the ground. The second "bump" is your foot hitting the ball.

YOUR GOAL: A score of 10 or more points

Today's Scores

	1	2	3	4	5	6	7	8	9	10	11	12	13	14	15	16	17	18	19	20	TOTAL
KICKS																					
HIT THE WALL																						

How To Watch Your Score Improve

1. Write down your score for today. The first day you do this drill, write your score by **DAY 1**, Write you score for the second day by **DAY 2**, and so on.

2. Did you meet your goal?

NO!

Erase **"Today's Scores"** and do this drill again the next time you **PRACTICE SOCCER BY YOURSELF.**

YES!

WELL DONE! The next time you **PRACTICE SOCCER BY YOURSELF** you can move up to the drill on the next page.

Also cut off the number on the top of this page. Then turn to the **PROGRESS CHART** at the end of the book.

DAY	SCORE
1	
2	
3	
4	
5	
6	
7	
8	
9	
10	

DAY	SCORE
11	
12	
13	
14	
15	
16	
17	
18	
19	
20	

DAY	SCORE
21	
22	
23	
24	
25	
26	
27	
28	
29	
30	

NOTES:

CLEARING HALF VOLLEY

What You Need To Do This Drill
- A small area of flat ground with a wall at one end
- A soccer ball
- A piece of chalk
- 2 markers (rags, sticks, cans, boxes, cones, etc.)
- This page, a pencil and an eraser

How To Set Up For This Drill

A. Place 2 markers 6 steps away from the wall. When you kick the ball you must be farther from the wall than the markers are.

B. Draw a line on the wall 6 large steps long and as high as the top of your head. You must kick the ball over this line.

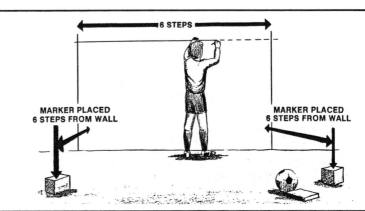

6 STEPS

MARKER PLACED 6 STEPS FROM WALL

MARKER PLACED 6 STEPS FROM WALL

How To Do This Drill

1. Stand facing the wall. Stand further from the wall than the markers.

2. Throw the ball straight up a little over your head.

3. Immediately after the ball hits the ground, kick the ball at the wall with the top (instep) of either foot. Kick the ball over the line.

4. Give yourself **1 point** if you kicked the ball after it bounced. Give yourself **1 more point** if the ball hit the wall over the line. Write down your points in **"Today's Scores."**

5. Do this drill 20 times.

6. After you have done the drill 20 times, add up your points. This is your score.

NOTE: Look at the ball as you kick it.

NOTE: To kick the ball high, bend your body backward away from the ball.

NOTE: To kick the ball high, kick it below its center point.

NOTE: Ball Bounces

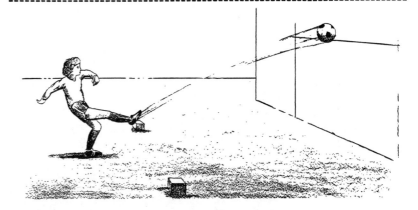

YOUR GOAL: A score of 20 or more points

Today's Scores

	1	2	3	4	5	6	7	8	9	10	11	12	13	14	15	16	17	18	19	20	TOTAL
KICKS																					
HIT THE WALL																						

How To Watch Your Score Improve

1. Write down your score for today. The first day you do this drill, write your score by **DAY 1**, Write you score for the second day by **DAY 2**, and so on.

2. Did you meet your goal?

NO!

Erase **"Today's Scores"** and do this drill again the next time you **PRACTICE SOCCER BY YOURSELF.**

YES!

WELL DONE! The next time you **PRACTICE SOCCER BY YOURSELF** you can move up to the drill on the next page.

Also cut off the number on the top of this page. Then turn to the **PROGRESS CHART** at the end of the book.

DAY	SCORE	DAY	SCORE	DAY	SCORE
1		11		21	
2		12		22	
3		13		23	
4		14		24	
5		15		25	
6		16		26	
7		17		27	
8		18		28	
9		19		29	
10		20		30	

NOTES:

CLEARING HALF VOLLEY WITH THE WEAKER FOOT

What You Need To Do This Drill

- A small area of flat ground with a wall at one end
- A soccer ball
- A piece of chalk
- 2 markers (rags, sticks, cans, boxes, cones, etc.)
- This page, a pencil and an eraser

How To Set Up For This Drill

A. Place 2 markers 6 steps away from the wall. When you kick the ball you must be farther from the wall than the markers are.

B. Draw a line on the wall 6 large steps long and as high as the top of your head. You must kick the ball over this line.

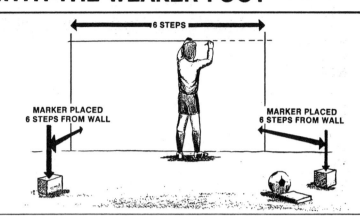

6 STEPS

MARKER PLACED
6 STEPS FROM WALL

MARKER PLACED
6 STEPS FROM WALL

How To Do This Drill

1. Stand facing the wall. Stand further from the wall than the markers.

2. Throw the ball straight up a little over your head.

3. Immediately after the ball hits the ground, kick the ball with the top (instep) of your weaker foot. Kick the ball over the line

4. Give yourself **1 point** if you kicked the ball immediately after it bounced. Give yourself **1 more point** if the ball hit the wall over the line. Write down your points in **"Today's Scores."**

5. Do this drill 20 times.

6. After you have done the drill 20 times, add up your points. This is your score.

NOTE: Look at the ball as you kick it.

NOTE: To kick the ball high, bend your body backward away from the ball.

NOTE: To kick the ball high, kick it below its center point.

NOTE: Ball Bounces

YOUR GOAL: A score of 10 or more points

Today's Scores

		1	2	3	4	5	6	7	8	9	10	11	12	13	14	15	16	17	18	19	20	
KICKS																							YOUR SCORE
HIT THE WALL																							

How To Watch Your Score Improve

1. Write down your score for today. The first day you do this drill, write your score by **DAY 1**, Write you score for the second day by **DAY 2**, and so on.

2. Did you meet your goal?

NO!

Erase **"Today's Scores"** and do this drill again the next time you **PRACTICE SOCCER BY YOURSELF.**

YES!

WELL DONE! The next time you **PRACTICE SOCCER BY YOURSELF** you can move up to the drill on the next page.

Also cut off the number on the top of this page. Then turn to the **PROGRESS CHART** at the end of the book.

DAY	SCORE	DAY	SCORE	DAY	SCORE
1		11		21	
2		12		22	
3		13		23	
4		14		24	
5		15		25	
6		16		26	
7		17		27	
8		18		28	
9		19		29	
10		20		30	

NOTES:

PASSING HALF VOLLEY

What You Need To Do This Drill
- A small area of flat ground with a wall at one end
- A soccer ball
- A piece of chalk
- 2 markers (rags, sticks, cans, boxes, cones, etc.)
- This page, a pencil and an eraser

How To Set Up For This Drill

A. Place 2 markers 6 steps away from the wall. When you kick the ball you must be farther from the wall than the markers are.

B Draw a line on the wall 6 large steps long and as high as your waist. You must kick the ball under the line.

6 STEPS

MARKER 6 STEPS FROM WALL

MARKER 6 STEPS FROM WALL

How To Do This Drill

1. Stand facing the wall. Stand further from the wall than the markers.

2. Throw the ball straight up a little over your head.

3. Immediately after the ball hits the ground, kick the ball at the wall with the inside of either foot. Kick the ball under the line.

4. Give yourself **1 point** if you kicked the ball immediately after it bounced. Give yourself **1 more point** if the ball hit the wall under the line. Write down your points in **"Today's Scores."**

5. Do this drill 20 times.

6. After you have done the drill 20 times, add up your points. This is your score.

NOTE: Ball Bounces

NOTE: Look at the ball as you kick it.

NOTE: To kick the ball low, bend your body forward over the ball.

NOTE: To kick the ball low, kick it at or above its center point.

YOUR GOAL: A score of 20 or more points

Today's Scores

	1	2	3	4	5	6	7	8	9	10	11	12	13	14	15	16	17	18	19	20	YOUR SCORE
KICKS																					
HIT THE WALL																					

How To Watch Your Score Improve

1. Write down your score for today. The first day you do this drill, write your score by **DAY 1**, Write you score for the second day by **DAY 2**, and so on.

2. Did you meet your goal?

NO!

Erase **"Today's Scores"** and do this drill again the next time you **PRACTICE SOCCER BY YOURSELF.**

YES!

WELL DONE! The next time you **PRACTICE SOCCER BY YOURSELF** you can move up to the drill on the next page.

Also cut off the number on the top of this page. Then turn to the **PROGRESS CHART** at the end of the book.

DAY	SCORE
1	
2	
3	
4	
5	
6	
7	
8	
9	
10	

DAY	SCORE
11	
12	
13	
14	
15	
16	
17	
18	
19	
20	

DAY	SCORE
21	
22	
23	
24	
25	
26	
27	
28	
29	
30	

NOTES:

PASSING HALF VOLLEY WITH THE WEAKER FOOT

What You Need To Do This Drill
- A small area of flat ground with a wall at one end
- A soccer ball
- A piece of chalk
- 2 markers (rags, sticks, cans, boxes, cones, etc.)
- This page, a pencil and an eraser

How To Set Up For This Drill
A. Place 2 markers 6 steps away from the wall. When you kick the ball you must be farther from the wall than the markers are.

B. Draw a line on the wall 6 large steps long and as high as your waist. You must kick the ball under this line.

MARKER 6 STEPS FROM WALL

6 STEPS

MARKER 6 STEPS FROM WALL

How To Do This Drill
1. Stand facing the wall. Stand further from the wall than the markers.

2. Throw the ball straight up a little over your head.

3. Immediately after the ball hits the ground, kick the ball at the wall with the inside your weaker foot. Kick the ball under the line.

4. Give yourself **1 point** if you kicked the ball immediately after it bounced. Give yourself **1 more point** if the ball hit the wall under the line. Write down your points in **"Today's Scores."**

5. Do this drill 20 times.

6. After you have done the drill 20 times, add up your points. This is your score.

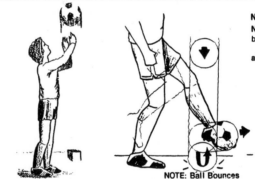

NOTE: Ball Bounces

NOTE: Look at the ball as you kick it.

NOTE: To kick the ball low, bend your body forward over the ball.
To kick the ball low, kick it at or above its center point.

YOUR GOAL: A score of 10 or more points

Today's Scores

	1	2	3	4	5	6	7	8	9	10	11	12	13	14	15	16	17	18	19	20	YOUR SCORE
KICKS																					
HIT THE WALL																						

How To Watch Your Score Improve

1. Write down your score for today. The first day you do this drill, write your score by **DAY 1**, Write you score for the second day by **DAY 2**, and so on.

2. Did you meet your goal?

NO!

Erase **"Today's Scores"** and do this drill again the next time you **PRACTICE SOCCER BY YOURSELF.**

YES!

WELL DONE! The next time you **PRACTICE SOCCER BY YOURSELF** you can move up to the drill on the next page.

Also cut off the number on the top of this page. Then turn to the **PROGRESS CHART** at the end of the book.

DAY	SCORE
1	
2	
3	
4	
5	
6	
7	
8	
9	
10	

DAY	SCORE
11	
12	
13	
14	
15	
16	
17	
18	
19	
20	

DAY	SCORE
21	
22	
23	
24	
25	
26	
27	
28	
29	
30	

NOTES:

PASSING HALF VOLLEY

What You Need To Do This Drill

- A small area of flat ground with a wall at one end
- A soccer ball
- A piece of chalk
- 2 markers (rags, sticks, cans, boxes, cones, etc.)
- This page, a pencil and an eraser

How To Set Up For This Drill

A. Place 2 markers 6 steps away from the wall. When you kick the ball you must be farther from the wall than the markers are.

B. Draw a line on the wall 6 large steps long and as high as your waist. You must kick the ball under this line.

6 STEPS

MARKER 6 STEPS FROM WALL

MARKER 6 STEPS FROM WALL

How To Do This Drill

1. Stand facing the wall. Stand further from the wall than the markers.

2. Throw the ball straight up a few feet over your head.

3. Immediately after the ball hits the ground, kick the ball at the wall with the inside of either foot. Kick the ball under the line.

4. Give yourself **1 point** if you kicked the ball immediately after it bounced. Give yourself **1 more point** if the ball hit the wall under the line. Write down your points in **"Today's Scores."**

5. Do this drill 20 times.

6. After you have done the drill 20 times, add up your points. This is your score.

NOTE. Look at the ball as you kick it.

NOTE: To kick the ball low, bend your body forward over the ball.

NOTE: To kick the ball low, kick it at or above its center point.

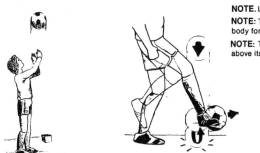

NOTE: Ball Bounces

YOUR GOAL: A score of 20 or more points

Today's Scores

	1	2	3	4	5	6	7	8	9	10	11	12	13	14	15	16	17	18	19	20	YOUR SCORE
KICKS																					
HIT THE WALL																					

How To Watch Your Score Improve

1. Write down your score for today. The first day you do this drill, write your score by **DAY 1**, Write you score for the second day by **DAY 2**, and so on.

2. Did you meet your goal?

NO!

Erase **"Today's Scores"** and do this drill again the next time you **PRACTICE SOCCER BY YOURSELF.**

YES!

WELL DONE! The next time you **PRACTICE SOCCER BY YOURSELF** you can move up to the drill on the next page.

Also cut off the number on the top of this page. Then turn to the **PROGRESS CHART** at the end of the book.

DAY	SCORE
1	
2	
3	
4	
5	
6	
7	
8	
9	
10	

DAY	SCORE
11	
12	
13	
14	
15	
16	
17	
18	
19	
20	

DAY	SCORE
21	
22	
23	
24	
25	
26	
27	
28	
29	
30	

NOTES:

PASSING HALF VOLLEY WITH THE WEAKER FOOT

What You Need To Do This Drill

- A small area of flat ground with a wall at one end
- A soccer ball
- A piece of chalk
- 2 markers (rags, sticks, cans, boxes, cones, etc.)
- This page, a pencil and an eraser

How To Set Up For This Drill

A. Place 2 markers 6 steps away from the wall. When you kick the ball you must be farther from the wall than the markers are.

B. Draw a line on the wall 6 large steps long and as high as your waist. You must kick the ball under this line.

6 STEPS

MARKER
6 STEPS
FROM WALL

MARKER
6 STEPS
FROM WALL

How To Do This Drill

1. Stand facing the wall. Stand further from the wall than the markers.

2. Throw the ball straight up a few feet over your head.

3. Immediately after the ball hits the ground, kick the ball with the inside of your weaker foot. Kick the ball under the line

4. Give yourself **1 point** if you kicked the ball immediately after it bounced. Give yourself **1 more point** if the ball hit the wall under the line. Write down your points in **"Today's Scores."**

5. Do this drill 20 times.

6. After you have done the drill 20 times, add up your points. This is your score.

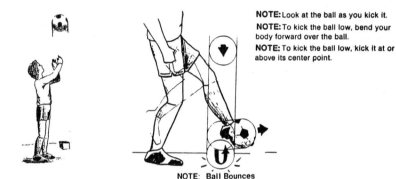

NOTE: Look at the ball as you kick it.

NOTE: To kick the ball low, bend your body forward over the ball.

NOTE: To kick the ball low, kick it at or above its center point.

NOTE: Ball Bounces

YOUR GOAL: A score of 10 or more points

Today's Scores

	1	2	3	4	5	6	7	8	9	10	11	12	13	14	15	16	17	18	19	20	YOUR SCORE
KICKS																					
HIT THE WALL																					

How To Watch Your Score Improve

1. Write down your score for today. The first day you do this drill, write your score by **DAY 1**, Write you score for the second day by **DAY 2**, and so on.

2. Did you meet your goal?

NO!

Erase **"Today's Scores"** and do this drill again the next time you **PRACTICE SOCCER BY YOURSELF.**

YES!

WELL DONE! The next time you **PRACTICE SOCCER BY YOURSELF** you can move up to the drill on the next page.

Also cut off the number on the top of this page. Then turn to the **PROGRESS CHART** at the end of the book.

DAY	SCORE	DAY	SCORE	DAY	SCORE
1		11		21	
2		12		22	
3		13		23	
4		14		24	
5		15		25	
6		16		26	
7		17		27	
8		18		28	
9		19		29	
10		20		30	

NOTES:

CLEARING FULL VOLLEY

What You Need To Do This Drill
- A small area of flat ground with a wall at one end
- A soccer ball
- A piece of chalk
- 2 markers (rags, sticks, cans, boxes, cones, etc.)
- This page, a pencil and an eraser

How To Set Up For This Drill

A. Place 2 markers 6 steps away from the wall. When you kick the ball you must be farther from the wall than the markers are.

B. Draw a line on the wall 6 large steps long and as high as the top of your head. You must kick the ball over this line.

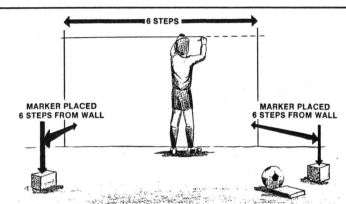

6 STEPS

MARKER PLACED 6 STEPS FROM WALL

MARKER PLACED 6 STEPS FROM WALL

How To Do This Drill

1. Stand facing the wall. Stand further from the wall than the markers.

2. Throw the ball straight up as high as you can over your head.

3. Before the ball hits the ground, kick the ball at the wall with the top (instep) of either foot.

4. Give yourself **1 point** if you kicked the ball before it bounced. Give yourself **1 more point** if the ball hit the wall over the line. Write down your points in **"Today's Scores."**

5. Do this drill 20 times.

6. After you have done the drill 20 times, add up your points. This is your score.

NOTE: Look at the ball as you kick it.

NOTE: To kick the ball high, bend your body backward away from the ball.

NOTE: To kick the ball high, kick it below its center point.

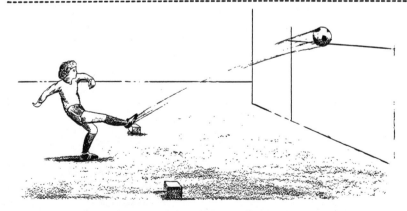

YOUR GOAL: A score of 30 or more points

Today's Scores

	1	2	3	4	5	6	7	8	9	10	11	12	13	14	15	16	17	18	19	20	YOUR SCORE
KICKS																					
HIT THE WALL																						

43

How To Watch Your Score Improve

1. Write down your score for today. The first day you do this drill, write your score by **DAY 1**, Write you score for the second day by **DAY 2**, and so on.

2. Did you meet your goal?

NO!

Erase **"Today's Scores"** and do this drill again the next time you **PRACTICE SOCCER BY YOURSELF.**

YES!

WELL DONE! The next time you **PRACTICE SOCCER BY YOURSELF** you can move up to the drill on the next page.

Also cut off the number on the top of this page. Then turn to the **PROGRESS CHART** at the end of the book.

DAY	SCORE
1	
2	
3	
4	
5	
6	
7	
8	
9	
10	

DAY	SCORE
11	
12	
13	
14	
15	
16	
17	
18	
19	
20	

DAY	SCORE
21	
22	
23	
24	
25	
26	
27	
28	
29	
30	

NOTES:

CLEARING FULL VOLLEY WITH THE WEAKER FOOT

What You Need To Do This Drill

- A small area of flat ground with a wall at one end
- A soccer ball
- A piece of chalk
- 2 markers (rags, sticks, cans, boxes, cones, etc.)
- This page, a pencil and an eraser

How To Set Up For This Drill

A. Place 2 markers 6 steps away from the wall. When you kick the ball you must be farther from the wall than the markers are.

B. Draw a line on the wall 6 large steps long and as high as the top of your head. You must kick the ball over this line.

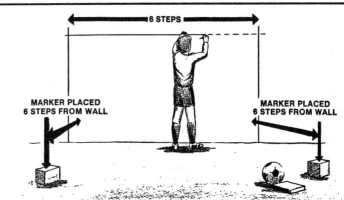

6 STEPS

MARKER PLACED 6 STEPS FROM WALL

MARKER PLACED 6 STEPS FROM WALL

How To Do This Drill

1. Stand facing the wall. Stand further from the wall than the markers.

2. Throw the ball straight up as high as you can over your head.

3. Before the ball hits the ground, kick the ball at the wall with the top (instep) of your weaker foot.

4. Give yourself **1 point** if you kicked the ball before it bounced. Give yourself **1 more point** if the ball hit the wall over the line. Write down your points in **"Today's Scores."**

5. Do this drill 20 times.

6. After you have done the drill 20 times, add up your points. This is your score.

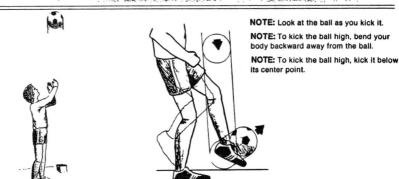

NOTE: Look at the ball as you kick it.

NOTE: To kick the ball high, bend your body backward away from the ball.

NOTE: To kick the ball high, kick it below its center point.

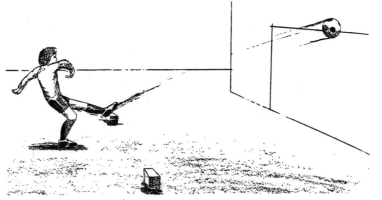

YOUR GOAL: A score of 20 or more points

Today's Scores

	1	2	3	4	5	6	7	8	9	10	11	12	13	14	15	16	17	18	19	20	YOUR SCORE
KICKS																					
HIT THE WALL																					

How To Watch Your Score Improve

1. Write down your score for today. The first day you do this drill, write your score by **DAY 1**, Write you score for the second day by **DAY 2**, and so on.

2. Did you meet your goal?

NO!

Erase **"Today's Scores"** and do this drill again the next time you **PRACTICE SOCCER BY YOURSELF.**

YES!

WELL DONE! The next time you **PRACTICE SOCCER BY YOURSELF** you can move up to the drill on the next page.

Also cut off the number on the top of this page. Then turn to the **PROGRESS CHART** at the end of the book.

DAY	SCORE
1	
2	
3	
4	
5	
6	
7	
8	
9	
10	

DAY	SCORE
11	
12	
13	
14	
15	
16	
17	
18	
19	
20	

DAY	SCORE
21	
22	
23	
24	
25	
26	
27	
28	
29	
30	

NOTES:

PASSING FULL VOLLEY

What You Need To Do This Drill
- A small area of flat ground with a wall at one end
- A soccer ball
- A piece of chalk
- 2 markers (rags, sticks, cans, boxes, cones, etc.)
- This page, a pencil and an eraser

How To Set Up For This Drill

A. Place 2 markers 6 steps away from the wall. When you kick the ball you must be farther from the wall than the markers are.

B. Draw a line on the wall 6 large steps long and as high as your waist. You must kick the ball under this line.

How To Do This Drill

1. Stand facing the wall. Stand further from the wall than the markers.

2. Throw the ball straight up as high as you can over your head.

3. Before the ball hits the ground, kick the ball at the wall with the inside of either foot. Kick the ball under the line.

4. Give yourself **1 point** if you kicked the ball before it bounced. Give yourself **1 more point** if the ball hit the wall under the line. Write down your points in **"Today's Scores."**

5. Do this drill 20 times.

6. After you have done the drill 20 times, add up your points. This is your score.

NOTE: Look at the ball as you kick it.

NOTE: To kick the ball low, bend your body forward over the ball.

NOTE: To kick the ball low, kick it at or above its center point.

YOUR GOAL: A score of 30 or more points

Today's Scores

		1	2	3	4	5	6	7	8	9	10	11	12	13	14	15	16	17	18	19	20	YOUR SCORE
KICKS																						
HIT THE WALL																						

How To Watch Your Score Improve

1. Write down your score for today. The first day you do this drill, write your score by **DAY 1**, Write you score for the second day by **DAY 2**, and so on.

2. Did you meet your goal?

NO!

Erase **"Today's Scores"** and do this drill again the next time you **PRACTICE SOCCER BY YOURSELF.**

YES!

WELL DONE! The next time you **PRACTICE SOCCER BY YOURSELF** you can move up to the drill on the next page.

Also cut off the number on the top of this page. Then turn to the **PROGRESS CHART** at the end of the book.

DAY	SCORE	DAY	SCORE	DAY	SCORE
1		11		21	
2		12		22	
3		13		23	
4		14		24	
5		15		25	
6		16		26	
7		17		27	
8		18		28	
9		19		29	
10		20		30	

NOTES:

PASSING FULL VOLLEY WITH THE WEAKER FOOT

What You Need To Do This Drill

- A small area of flat ground with a wall at one end
- A soccer ball
- A piece of chalk
- 2 markers (rags, sticks, cans, boxes, cones, etc.)
- This page, a pencil and an eraser

How To Set Up For This Drill

A. Place 2 markers 6 steps away from the wall. When you kick the ball you must be farther from the wall than the markers are.

B. Draw a line on the wall 6 large steps long and as high as your waist. You must kick the ball under this line.

6 STEPS

MARKER 6 STEPS FROM WALL

MARKER 6 STEPS FROM WALL

How To Do This Drill

1. Stand facing the wall. Stand further from the wall than the markers.

2. Throw the ball straight up as high as you can over your head.

3. Immediately after the ball hits the ground, kick the ball at the wall with the inside of either foot. Kick the ball under the line.

4. Give yourself **1 point** if you kicked the ball before it bounced. Give yourself **1 more point** if the ball hit the wall under the line. Write down your points in **"Today's Scores."**

5. Do this drill 20 times.

6. After you have done the drill 20 times, add up your points. This is your score.

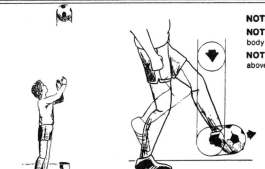

NOTE: Look at the ball as you kick it.

NOTE: To kick the ball low, bend your body forward over the ball.

NOTE: To kick the ball low, kick it at or above its center point.

YOUR GOAL: A score of 20 or more points

Today's Scores

	1	2	3	4	5	6	7	8	9	10	11	12	13	14	15	16	17	18	19	20	TOTAL
KICKS																					
HIT THE WALL																					

How To Watch Your Score Improve

1. Write down your score for today. The first day you do this drill, write your score by **DAY 1**, Write you score for the second day by **DAY 2**, and so on.

2. Did you meet your goal?

NO!

Erase **"Today's Scores"** and do this drill again the next time you **PRACTICE SOCCER BY YOURSELF.**

YES!

WELL DONE! The next time you **PRACTICE SOCCER BY YOURSELF** you can move up to the drill on the next page.

Also cut off the number on the top of this page. Then turn to the **PROGRESS CHART** at the end of the book.

DAY	SCORE
1	
2	
3	
4	
5	
6	
7	
8	
9	
10	

DAY	SCORE
11	
12	
13	
14	
15	
16	
17	
18	
19	
20	

DAY	SCORE
21	
22	
23	
24	
25	
26	
27	
28	
29	
30	

NOTES:

Why Should You Practice...

. . .SHOOTING?

Picture yourself in a soccer game. You have just dribbled the ball by the other team's player who was guarding you. Only the goalie stands between you and the goal.

Now, think about what you might do.

You can shoot the ball at the "near" side of the goal, but the goalie is in your way. You can shoot the ball at the far side of the goal, but you would have to kick the ball hard and with good control so the goalie can't get it.

You've been practicing your shooting by yourself. You turn, look at the far side of the goal, look down at the ball and take a hard shot at the far side.

The goalie is good, and gets a hand out and hits the ball.

As the ball bounces away from the goal, you run up and hit the ball into the corner.

Well done!

Some tips for good shooting:

1. Shoot for the far side of the goal.

2. Always follow the ball after the shot.

3. Unless you are taking a long shot, try to kick the ball low, or on the ground.

SET SHOT AT THE FAR SIDE

What You Need To Do This Drill

- A small area of flat ground with a wall at one end
- A soccer ball
- 2 markers (rags, paper, cup tops, etc.)
- A piece of chalk
- This page, a pencil and an eraser

How To Set Up For This Drill

A. Draw a small goal on the wall. It should be as high as you can reach and 6 large steps wide.

B. Draw targets at the left and right ends of the goal. Each target should be 2 steps wide and go from the ground to the top of the goal.

C. Place a marker 6 large steps out from the left end of the goal. Place another marker 6 large steps out from the right end of the goal.

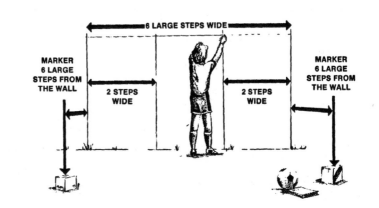

How To Do This Drill

1. Set the ball near the marker on the right side of the goal. Stand facing the goal.

2. Use your right foot to kick the ball at the target on the left side of the goal.

3. Then run and touch the spot where the ball hit the wall.

4. Give yourself **2 points** if the ball hit the target. Give yourself **1 more point** if you remembered to touch the spot where the ball hit the wall.

5. Write down your points in **"Today's Scores (Part 1)."**

6. Do this drill 10 times and count up your points in **"(Part 1)."**   **GO TO THE NEXT PAGE**

NOTE: Look at the goal, then look down at the ball as you kick it.

NOTE: Kick the ball at or above its midpoint, with the top of your foot. Your toe should be pointing down.

NOTE: Your body and knee should be over the ball when you kick it. This will keep your shot low.

NOTE: The foot you are not using to kick the ball should be beside the ball as you kick it.

NOTE: Running up to the wall after the shot will help you learn to run up for rebound shots. Rebound shots happen when the ball bounces off the goalpost and when the goalkeeper hits the ball away from the goal.

Today's Scores PART 1

HIT THE TARGET 2 POINTS											
RUN 1 POINT											

=

SCORE PART 1

7. Set the ball near the marker on the left side of the goal. Stand facing the goal.

8. Use your left foot to kick the ball at the target on the right side of the goal.

9. Then run and touch the spot where the ball hit the wall.

10. Give yourself **2 points** if you hit the target. Give yourself **1 more point** if you remembered to touch the spot where the ball hit the wall.

11. Write down your points in **"Today's Scores (Part 2)."**

. Do this drill 10 times and count up your points in **"(Part 2)."**

13. Add up your points for **"Today's Score (Part 1)" plus "(Part 2)."** This is your score.

NOTE: Look at the goal, then look down at the ball as you kick it.

NOTE: Kick the ball at or above its midpoint, with the top of your foot. Your toe should be pointing down.

NOTE: Your body and knee should be over the ball when you kick it. This will keep your shot low.

NOTE: The foot you are not using to kick the ball should be beside the ball as you kick it.

Today's Scores   PART 2

YOUR GOAL: A score of 30 or more points

HIT THE TARGET 2 POINTS										
RUN 1 POINT										

$=$
PART 1
$+$
PART 2
$=$
SCORE

How To Watch Your Scores Improve

1. Write down your score for today. The first day you do this drill, write your score by **DAY 1**, Write you score for the second day by **DAY 2**, and so on.

2. Did you meet your goal?

NO!

Erase **"Today's Scores"** and do this drill again the next time you **PRACTICE SOCCER BY YOURSELF.**

YES!

WELL DONE! The next time you **PRACTICE SOCCER BY YOURSELF** you can move up to the drill on the next page.

Also cut off the number on the top of this page. Then turn to the **PROGRESS CHART** at the end of the book.

DAY	SCORE	DAY	SCORE	DAY	SCORE
1		11		21	
2		12		22	
3		13		23	
4		14		24	
5		15		25	
6		16		26	
7		17		27	
8		18		28	
9		19		29	
10		20		30	

BALL ROLLING TO THE FAR POST, SHOT AT FAR SIDE

What You Need To Do This Drill
- A small area of flat ground with a wall at one end
- A soccer ball
- 3 markers (rags, paper, cup tops, etc.)
- A piece of chalk
- This page, a pencil and an eraser

How to Set Up For This Drill
A. Draw a small goal on the wall. It should be as high as you can reach and 6 large steps wide.

B. Draw targets at the left and right ends of the goal. Each target should be 2 steps wide and go from the ground to the top of the goal.

C. Place a marker 8 large steps out from the left end of the goal. Place another marker 8 large steps out from the right end of the goal. Place a third marker 6 large steps out from the center of the goal.

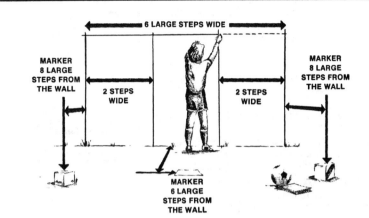

How To Do This Drill
1. Set the ball near the marker on the right side of the goal. Stand facing the goal.

2. Roll the ball (with either foot) toward the left side of the goal.

3. Then use your left foot to kick the ball at the target on the left side of the goal. Kick the ball before it is closer to the wall than the center marker.

4. Finally run and touch the spot where the ball hit the wall

5. Give yourself **2 points** if the ball hit the target. Give yourself **1 more point** if you remembered to touch the spot where the ball hit the wall.

6. Write down your points in **"Today's Scores (Part 1)."**

7. Do this drill 10 times and count up your points in **"(Part 1)."**   **GO TO THE NEXT PAGE**

NOTE: Look at the goal, then look down at the ball as you kick it.

NOTE: Kick the ball at or above its midpoint, with the top of your foot. Your toe should be pointing down.

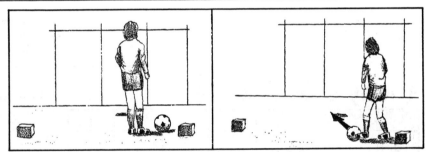

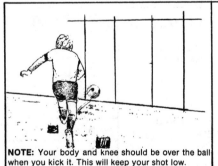

NOTE: Your body and knee should be over the ball when you kick it. This will keep your shot low.

NOTE: The foot you are not using to kick the ball should be beside the ball as you kick it.

Today's Scores PART 1

											SCORE PART 1
HIT THE TARGET 2 POINTS											=
RUN 1 POINT											

BALL ROLLING TO THE FAR POST,
SHOT AT THE FAR SIDE (CONTINUED)

8. Set the ball near the marker on the left side of the goal. Stand facing the goal.

9. Roll the ball (with either foot) towards the right side of the goal.

10. The use your right foot to kick the ball at the target on the right side of the goal. Kick the ball before it is closer to the wall than the center marker.

11. Finally, run and touch the spot where the ball hit the wall.

12. Give yourself **2 points** if you hit the target. Give yourself **1 more point** if you remembered to touch the spot where the ball hit the wall.

13. Write down your points in **"Today's Scores.**

14. Do this drill 10 times and count up your points in **"(Part 2)."**

15. Add up your points for **"Today's Score (Part 1)"** plus **"(Part 2)."** This is your score.

Today's Scores   PART 2

YOUR GOAL: A score of 30 or more points

HIT THE TARGET 2 POINTS										
RUN 1 POINT										

=   **PART 1** ☐   +   **PART 2** ☐   =   **SCORE** ☐

How To Watch Your Scores Improve

1. Write down your score for today. The first day you do this drill, write your score by **DAY 1**, Write you score for the second day by **DAY 2**, and so on.

2. Did you meet your goal?

NO!

Erase **"Today's Scores"** and do this drill again the next time you **PRACTICE SOCCER BY YOURSELF.**

YES!

WELL DONE! The next time you **PRACTICE SOCCER BY YOURSELF** you can move up to the drill on the next page.

Also cut off the number on the top of this page. Then turn to the **PROGRESS CHART** at the end of the book.

DAY	SCORE	DAY	SCORE	DAY	SCORE
1		11		21	
2		12		22	
3		13		23	
4		14		24	
5		15		25	
6		16		26	
7		17		27	
8		18		28	
9		19		29	
10		20		30	

BALL ROLLING TO THE NEAR POST, SHOT AT THE FAR SIDE

What You Need To Do This Drill

- A small area of flat ground with a wall at one end
- A soccer ball
- 3 markers (rags, paper, cup tops, etc.)
- A piece of chalk
- This page, a pencil and an eraser

How to Set Up For This Drill

A. Draw a small goal on the wall. It should be as high as you can reach and 6 large steps wide.

B. Draw targets at the left and right ends of the goal. Each target should be 2 steps wide and go from the ground to the top of the goal.

C. Place a marker 8 large steps out from the left end of the goal. Place another marker 8 large steps out from the right end of the goal. Place a third marker 6 large steps out from the center of the goal.

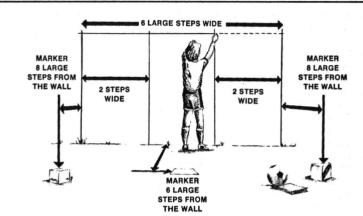

How To Do This Drill

1. Set the ball near the marker on the right side of the goal. Stand facing the goal.

2. Roll the ball (with either foot) toward the right side of the goal.

3. Then use your right foot to kick the ball at the target on the left side of the goal. Kick the ball before it is closer to the wall than the center marker.

4. Finally run and touch the spot where the ball hit the wall

5. Give yourself **2 points** if the ball hit the target. Give yourself **1 more point** if you remembered to touch the spot where the ball hit the wall.

6. Write down your points in **"Today's Scores (Part 1)."**

7. Do this drill 10 times and count up your points in **"(Part 1)."**   **GO TO THE NEXT PAGE**

NOTE: Look at the goal, then look down at the ball as you kick it.

NOTE: Kick the ball at or above its midpoint, with the top of your foot. Your toe should be pointing down.

NOTE: Your body and knee should be over the ball when you kick it. This will keep your shot low.

NOTE: The foot you are not using to kick the ball should be beside the ball as you kick it.

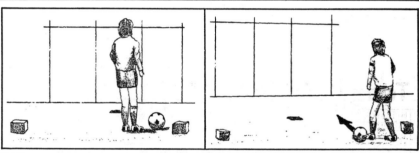

Today's Scores PART 1

											SCORE PART 1
HIT THE TARGET 2 POINTS											
RUN 1 POINT											=

BALL ROLLING TO THE NEAR POST, SHOT AT THE FAR SIDE (Continued)

8. Set the ball near the marker on the left side of the goal. Stand facing the goal.

9. Roll the ball (with either foot) towards the left side of the goal.

10. Then use your left foot to kick the ball at the target on the right side of the goal. Kick the ball before it is closer to the wall than the center marker.

11. Finally, run and touch the spot where the ball hit the wall.

12. Give yourself **2 points** if you hit the target. Give yourself **1 more point** if you remembered to run immediately and touch the spot where the ball hit the wall.

13. Write down your points in **"Today's Scores (Part 2)."**

14. Do this drill 10 times and count up your points in **"(Part 2)."**

15. Add up your points for **"Today's Score (Part 1)" plus "(Part 2)."** This is your score.

Today's Scores PART 2

YOUR GOAL: A score of 30 or more points

HIT THE TARGET 2 POINTS										
RUN 1 POINT										

= [PART 1] + [PART 2] = [SCORE]

How To Watch Your Scores Improve

1. Write down your score for today. The first day you do this drill, write your score by **DAY 1**, Write you score for the second day by **DAY 2**, and so on.

2. Did you meet your goal?

NO!

Erase **"Today's Scores"** and do this drill again the next time you **PRACTICE SOCCER BY YOURSELF.**

YES!

WELL DONE! The next time you **PRACTICE SOCCER BY YOURSELF** you can move up to the drill on the next page.

Also cut off the number on the top of this page. Then turn to the **PROGRESS CHART** at the end of the book.

DAY	SCORE	DAY	SCORE	DAY	SCORE
1		11		21	
2		12		22	
3		13		23	
4		14		24	
5		15		25	
6		16		26	
7		17		27	
8		18		28	
9		19		29	
10		20		30	

BALL BOUNCING TO THE FAR POST, SHOT AT THE FAR SIDE

What You Need To Do This Drill

- A small area of flat ground with a wall at one end
- A soccer ball
- 3 markers (rags, paper, cup tops, etc.)
- A piece of chalk
- This page, a pencil and an eraser

How to Set Up For This Drill

A. Draw a small goal on the wall. It should be as high as you can reach and 6 large steps wide.

B. Draw targets at the left and right ends of the goal. Each target should be 2 steps wide and go from the ground to the top of the goal.

C. Place a marker 8 large steps out from the left end of the goal. Place another marker 8 large steps out from the right end of the goal. Place a third marker 6 large steps out from the center of the goal.

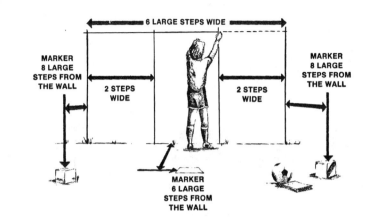

How To Do This Drill

1. Stand with the ball near the marker on the right side of the goal. Stand facing the goal.

2. Bounce the ball towards the left side of the goal.

3. Then use your left foot to kick the ball at the target on the left side of the goal. Kick the ball before it bounces twice and before it is closer to the wall than the center marker

4. Finally run and touch the spot where the ball hit the wall

5. Give yourself **2 points** if the ball hit the target. Give yourself **1 more point** if you remembered to touch the spot where the ball hit the wall.

6. Write down your points in **"Today's Scores (Part 1)."**

7. Do this drill 10 times and count up your points in **"(Part 1)."**

> **NOTE:** Look at the goal, then look down at the ball as you kick it.
>
> **NOTE:** Kick the ball at or above its midpoint, with the top of your foot. Your toe should be pointing down.
>
> **NOTE:** Your body and knee should be over the ball when you kick it. This will keep your shot low.
>
> **NOTE:** The foot you are not using to kick the ball should be beside the ball as you kick it.

Today's Scores PART 1

HIT THE TARGET 2 POINTS										
RUN 1 POINT										

=

SCORE PART 1

BALL BOUNCING TO THE FAR POST,
SHOT AT THE FAR SIDE (Continued)

8. Stand with the ball near the marker on the left side of the goal. Stand facing the goal.

9. Bounce the ball towards the right side of the goal.

10. Then use your right foot to kick the ball at the target on the right side of the goal. Kick the ball before it bounces twice and before it is closer to the wall than the center marker.

11. Finally, run and touch the spot where the ball hit the wall.

12. Give yourself **2 points** if you hit the target. Give yourself **1 more point** if you remembered to run immediately and touch the spot where the ball hit the wall.

13. Write down your points in **"Today's Scores (Part 2)."**

14. Do this drill 10 times and count up your points in **"(Part 2)."**

15. Add up your points for **"Today's Score (Part 1)" plus "(Part 2)."** This is your score.

Today's Scores PART 2

YOUR GOAL: A score of 30 or more points

HIT THE TARGET 2 POINTS										
RUN 1 POINT										

$$= \boxed{} + \boxed{} = \boxed{}$$

PART 1   PART 2   SCORE

How To Watch Your Scores Improve

1. Write down your score for today. The first day you do this drill, write your score by **DAY 1**, Write you score for the second day by **DAY 2**, and so on.

2. Did you meet your goal?

NO!

Erase **"Today's Scores"** and do this drill again the next time you **PRACTICE SOCCER BY YOURSELF.**

YES!

WELL DONE! The next time you **PRACTICE SOCCER BY YOURSELF** you can move up to the drill on the next page.

Also cut off the number on the top of this page. Then turn to the **PROGRESS CHART** at the end of the book.

DAY	SCORE
1	
2	
3	
4	
5	
6	
7	
8	
9	
10	

DAY	SCORE
11	
12	
13	
14	
15	
16	
17	
18	
19	
20	

DAY	SCORE
21	
22	
23	
24	
25	
26	
27	
28	
29	
30	

BALL BOUNCING TO THE NEAR POST, SHOT AT THE FAR SIDE

What You Need To Do This Drill

- A small area of flat ground with a wall at one end
- A soccer ball
- 3 markers (rags, paper, cup tops, etc.)
- A piece of chalk
- This page, a pencil and an eraser

How to Set Up For This Drill

A. Draw a small goal on the wall. It should be as high as you can reach and 6 large steps wide.

B. Draw targets at the left and right ends of the goal. Each target should be 2 steps wide and go from the ground to the top of the goal.

C. Place a marker 8 large steps out from the left end of the goal. Place another marker 8 large steps out from the right end of the goal. Place a third marker 6 large steps out from the center of the goal.

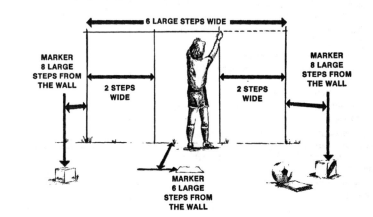

6 LARGE STEPS WIDE

MARKER 8 LARGE STEPS FROM THE WALL

2 STEPS WIDE

2 STEPS WIDE

MARKER 8 LARGE STEPS FROM THE WALL

MARKER 6 LARGE STEPS FROM THE WALL

How To Do This Drill

1. Stand with the ball near the marker on the right side of the goal. Stand facing the goal.

2. Bounce the ball towards the right side of the goal.

3. Then use your right foot to kick the ball at the target on the left side of the goal. Kick the ball before it bounces twice and before it is closer to the wall than the center marker

4. Finally run and touch the spot where the ball hit the wall

5. Give yourself **2 points** if the ball hit the target. Give yourself **1 more point** if you remembered to touch the spot where the ball hit the wall.

6. Write down your points in **"Today's Scores (Part 1)."**

7. Do this drill 10 times and count up your points in **"(Part 1)."** **GO TO THE NEXT PAGE**

> **NOTE:** Look at the goal, then look down at the ball as you kick it.
> **NOTE:** Kick the ball at or above its midpoint, with the top of your foot. Your toe should be pointing down.
> **NOTE:** Your body and knee should be over the ball when you kick it. This will keep your shot low.
> **NOTE:** The foot you are not using to kick the ball should be beside the ball as you kick it.

Today's Scores PART 1

HIT THE TARGET 2 POINTS										
RUN 1 POINT										

SCORE PART 1

=

BALL BOUNCING TO THE NEAR POST, SHOT AT THE FAR SIDE (Continued)

8. Stand with the ball near the marker on the left side of the goal. Stand facing the goal.

9. Bounce the ball towards the left side of the goal.

10. Then use your left foot to kick the ball at the target on the right side of the goal. Kick the ball before it bounces twice and before it is closer to the wall than the center marker.

11. Finally, run and touch the spot where the ball hit the wall.

12. Give yourself **2 points** if you hit the target. Give yourself **1 more point** if you remembered to run immediately and touch the spot where the ball hit the wall.

13. Write down your points in **"Today's Scores (Part 2)."**

14. Do this drill 10 times and count up your points in **"(Part 2)."**

15. Add up your points for **"Today's Score (Part 1)" plus "(Part 2)."** This is your score.

Today's Scores PART 2

YOUR GOAL: A score of 30 or more points

HIT THE TARGET 2 POINTS										
RUN 1 POINT										

= | PART 1 | + | PART 2 | = | SCORE |

How To Watch Your Scores Improve

1. Write down your score for today. The first day you do this drill, write your score by **DAY 1**, Write you score for the second day by **DAY 2**, and so on.

2. Did you meet your goal?

NO!

Erase **"Today's Scores"** and do this drill again the next time you **PRACTICE SOCCER BY YOURSELF.**

YES!

WELL DONE! The next time you **PRACTICE SOCCER BY YOURSELF** you can move up to the drill on the next page.

Also cut off the number on the top of this page. Then turn to the **PROGRESS CHART** at the end of the book.

DAY	SCORE	DAY	SCORE	DAY	SCORE
1		11		21	
2		12		22	
3		13		23	
4		14		24	
5		15		25	
6		16		26	
7		17		27	
8		18		28	
9		19		29	
10		20		30	

BALL BOUNCING TO THE FAR POST, TURN AROUND SHOT AT THE FAR SIDE

What You Need To Do This Drill

- A small area of flat ground with a wall at one end
- A soccer ball
- 3 markers (rags, paper, cup tops, etc.)
- A piece of chalk
- This page, a pencil and an eraser

How to Set Up For This Drill

A. Draw a small goal on the wall. It should be as high as you can reach and 6 large steps wide.

B. Draw targets at the left and right ends of the goal. Each target should be 2 steps wide and go from the ground to the top of the goal.

C. Place a marker 8 large steps out from the left end of the goal. Place another marker 8 large steps out from the right end of the goal. Place a third marker 6 large steps out from the center of the goal.

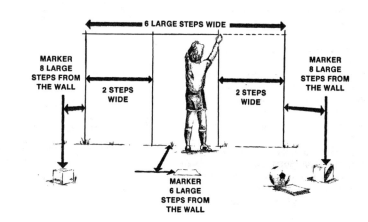

How To Do This Drill

1. Stand with the ball near the marker on the right side of the goal. Stand with your back to goal.

2. Throw the ball gently over your head towards the left side of the goal.

3. Turn around. Use your left foot to kick the ball at the target on the left side of the goal. Kick the ball before it bounces twice and before it is closer to the wall than the center marker

4. Finally run and touch the spot where the ball hit the wall

5. Give yourself **2 points** if the ball hit the target. Give yourself **1 more point** if you remembered to touch the spot where the ball hit the wall.

6. Write down your points in **"Today's Scores (Part 1)."**

7. Do this drill 10 times and count up your points in **"(Part 1)."**   **GO TO THE NEXT PAGE**

NOTE: Look at the goal, then look down at the ball as you kick it.

NOTE: Kick the ball at or above its midpoint, with the top of your foot. Your toe should be pointing down.

NOTE: Your body and knee should be over the ball when you kick it. This will keep your shot low.

NOTE: The foot you are not using to kick the ball should be beside the ball as you kick it.

Today's Scores PART 1

HIT THE TARGET 2 POINTS										
RUN 1 POINT										

SCORE PART 1

=

BALL BOUNCING TO THE FAR POST, TURN AROUND SHOT AT THE FAR SIDE (Continued)

8. Stand with the ball near the marker on the left side of the goal. Stand with your back to the goal.

9. Throw the ball gently over your head towards the right side of the goal.

10. Turn around. Use your right foot to kick the ball at the target on the right side of the goal. Kick the ball before it bounces twice and before it is closer to the wall than the center marker.

11. Finally, run and touch the spot where the ball hit the wall.

12. Give yourself **2 points** if you hit the target. Give yourself **1 more point** if you remembered to run immediately and touch the spot where the ball hit the wall.

13. Write down your points in **"Today's Scores (Part 2)."**

14. Do this drill 10 times and count up your points in **"(Part 2)."**

15. Add up your points for **"Today's Score (Part 1)" plus "(Part 2)."** This is your score.

NOTE: Look at the goal, then look down at the ball as you kick it.

Today's Scores PART 2

YOUR GOAL: A score of 30 or more points

HIT THE TARGET 2 POINTS										
RUN 1 POINT										

$$= \boxed{} + \boxed{} = \boxed{}$$

PART 1	PART 2	SCORE

How To Watch Your Scores Improve

1. Write down your score for today. The first day you do this drill, write your score by **DAY 1**, Write you score for the second day by **DAY 2**, and so on.

2. Did you meet your goal?

NO!

Erase **"Today's Scores"** and do this drill again the next time you **PRACTICE SOCCER BY YOURSELF.**

YES!

WELL DONE! The next time you **PRACTICE SOCCER BY YOURSELF** you can move up to the drill on the next page.

Also cut off the number on the top of this page. Then turn to the **PROGRESS CHART** at the end of the book.

DAY	SCORE	DAY	SCORE	DAY	SCORE
1		11		21	
2		12		22	
3		13		23	
4		14		24	
5		15		25	
6		16		26	
7		17		27	
8		18		28	
9		19		29	
10		20		30	

BALL BOUNCING TO THE NEAR POST, TURN AROUND SHOT AT THE FAR SIDE

What You Need To Do This Drill

- A small area of flat ground with a wall at one end
- A soccer ball
- 3 markers (rags, paper, cup tops, etc.)
- A piece of chalk
- This page, a pencil and an eraser

How to Set Up For This Drill

A. Draw a small goal on the wall. It should be as high as you can reach and 6 large steps wide.

B. Draw targets at the left and right ends of the goal. Each target should be 2 steps wide and go from the ground to the top of the goal.

C. Place a marker 8 large steps out from the left end of the goal. Place another marker 8 large steps out from the right end of the goal. Place a third marker 6 large steps out from the center of the goal.

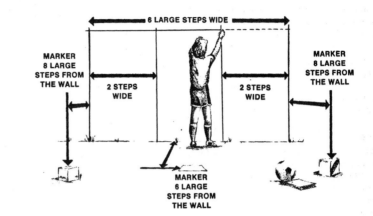

How To Do This Drill

1. Stand with the ball near the marker on the right side of the goal. Stand with your back to goal.

2. Throw the ball gently over your head towards the right side of the goal.

3. Then turn around. Use your right foot to kick the ball at the target on the left side of the goal. Kick the ball before it bounces twice and before it is closer to the wall than the center marker

4. Finally run and touch the spot where the ball hit the wall

5. Give yourself **2 points** if the ball hit the target. Give yourself **1 more point** if you remembered to touch the spot where the ball hit the wall.

6. Write down your points in **"Today's Scores (Part 1)."**

7. Do this drill 10 times and count up your points in **"(Part 1)."**   **GO TO THE NEXT PAGE**

NOTE: Look at the goal, then look down at the ball as you kick it.

NOTE: Kick the ball at or above its midpoint, with the top of your foot. Your toe should be pointing down.

NOTE: Your body and knee should be over the ball when you kick it. This will keep your shot low.

NOTE: The foot you are not using to kick the ball should be beside the ball as you kick it.

Today's Scores PART 1

HIT THE TARGET 2 POINTS												
RUN 1 POINT												

= **SCORE PART 1** [ ]

BALL BOUNCING TO THE NEAR POST,
TURN AROUND SHOT AT THE FAR SIDE (Continued)

8. Stand with the ball near the marker on the left side of the goal. Stand with your back to the goal.

9. Throw the ball gently over your head towards the left side of the goal.

10. Then turn around. Use your left foot to kick the ball at the target on the right side of the goal. Kick the ball before it bounces twice and before it is closer to the wall than the center marker.

11. Finally, run and touch the spot where the ball hit the wall.

12. Give yourself **2 points** if you hit the target. Give yourself **1 more point** if you remembered to run immediately and touch the spot where the ball hit the wall.

13. Write down your points in **"Today's Scores (Part 2)."**

14. Do this drill 10 times and count up your points in **"(Part 2)."**

15. Add up your points for **"Today's Score (Part 1)" plus "(Part 2)."** This is your score.

Today's Scores PART 2

HIT THE TARGET 2 POINTS										
RUN 1 POINT										

YOUR GOAL: A score of 30 or more points

	PART 1		PART 2		SCORE
=		+		=	

How To Watch Your Scores Improve

1. Write down your score for today. The first day you do this drill, write your score by **DAY 1**, Write you score for the second day by **DAY 2**, and so on.

2. Did you meet your goal?

NO!

Erase **"Today's Scores"** and do this drill again the next time you **PRACTICE SOCCER BY YOURSELF.**

YES!

WELL DONE! The next time you **PRACTICE SOCCER BY YOURSELF** you can move up to the drill on the next page.

Also cut off the number on the top of this page. Then turn to the **PROGRESS CHART** at the end of the book.

DAY	SCORE	DAY	SCORE	DAY	SCORE
1		11		21	
2		12		22	
3		13		23	
4		14		24	
5		15		25	
6		16		26	
7		17		27	
8		18		28	
9		19		29	
10		20		30	

HEAD SHOOTING

What You Need To Do This Drill

- A small area of flat ground with a wall at one end
- A soccer ball
- 1 marker (rags, paper, cup tops, etc.)
- A piece of chalk
- This page, a pencil and an eraser

How to Set Up For This Drill

A. Draw a small goal on the wall. It should be as high as you can reach and 6 large steps wide.

B. Draw targets at the left and right ends of the goal. Each target should be 2 steps wide and go from the ground to the top of the goal.

C. Place a marker 3 large steps out from the center of the goal.

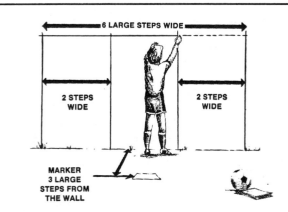

6 LARGE STEPS WIDE

2 STEPS WIDE

2 STEPS WIDE

MARKER 3 LARGE STEPS FROM THE WALL

How To Do This Drill

1. Stand with the ball on the side of, and behind the center marker. Do steps 1-6 10 times from the right side of the center marker and 10 times from the left.

2. Throw the ball high up on the wall, straight in front of you.

3. When the ball bounces off the wall, head the ball towards the target on the left. Hit the ball only once.

4. Finally run and touch the spot where the ball hit the wall.

5. Give yourself **2 points** if the ball hit the target. Give yourself **1 more point** if you remembered to touch the spot where the ball hit the wall.

6. Write down your points in **"Today's Scores (Part 1)."**

7. Do steps 1-6 20 times. Ten times starting from the right side of the center marker and heading at the left target. Ten times from the left side of the center marker and heading the right target.

8. Add up your points in **"Today's Scores."** This is your score.

NOTE: When you hit the ball with your head:

a. be sure to hit the ball with the top of your forehead. Hitting the ball with the your head won't hurt if you use your forehead.

b. keep your eyes open and watch the ball as your head hits it.

c. keep your mouth closed.

d. swing your body from the waist to get good power.

NOTE: To head the ball down, your forehead should hit the ball above its centerline and you should "snap" your head downward as you hit the ball.

YOUR GOAL: A score of 30 or more points

Today's Scores

	1	2	3	4	5	6	7	8	9	10	11	12	13	14	15	16	17	18	19	20	TOTAL
HIT THE TARGET 2 POINTS																					
RUN 1 POINT																					

How To Watch Your Score Improve

1. Write down your score for today. The first day you do this drill, write your score by **DAY 1**, Write you score for the second day by **DAY 2**, and so on.

2. Did you meet your goal?

NO!

Erase **"Today's Scores"** and do this drill again the next time you **PRACTICE SOCCER BY YOURSELF.**

YES!

WELL DONE! The next time you **PRACTICE SOCCER BY YOURSELF** you can move up to the drill on the next page.

Also cut off the number on the top of this page. Then turn to the **PROGRESS CHART** at the end of the book.

DAY	SCORE	DAY	SCORE	DAY	SCORE
1		11		21	
2		12		22	
3		13		23	
4		14		24	
5		15		25	
6		16		26	
7		17		27	
8		18		28	
9		19		29	
10		20		30	

NOTES:

BALL ROLLING TO MID-GOAL, SHOT AT THE SIDE

What You Need To Do This Drill

- A small area of flat ground with a wall at one end
- A soccer ball
- 3 markers (rags, paper, cup tops, etc.)
- A piece of chalk
- This page, a pencil and an eraser

How to Set Up For This Drill

A. Draw a small goal on the wall. It should be as high as you can reach and 6 large steps wide.

B. Draw targets at the left and right ends of the goal. Each target should be 2 steps wide and go from the ground to the top of the goal.

C. Place a marker 6 large steps out from the left end of the goal. Place another marker 6 large steps out from the right end of the goal. Place a third marker 8 large steps out from the center of the goal.

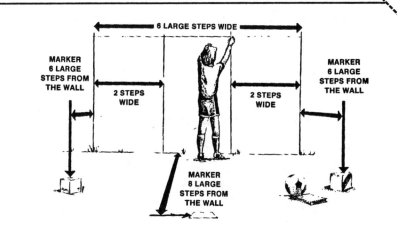

How To Do This Drill

1. Set the ball near the center marker. Stand facing the goal.

2. Roll the ball (with either foot) toward the middle of the goal.

3. Then use your right foot to kick the ball at the target on the left side of the goal. Kick the ball before it is closer to the wall than the right and left markers.

4. Finally run and touch the spot where the ball hit the wall

5. Give yourself **2 points** if the ball hit the target. Give yourself **1 more point** if you remembered to touch the spot where the ball hit the wall.

6. Write down your points in **"Today's Scores (Part 1)."**

7. Do this drill 10 times and count up your points in **"(Part 1)."**   **GO TO THE NEXT PAGE**

Today's Scores PART 1

HIT THE TARGET 2 POINTS										
RUN 1 POINT										

SCORE PART 1

=

BALL ROLLING TO MID-GOAL, SHOT AT THE SIDE (Continued)

8. Set the ball near the center marker. Stand facing the goal.

9. Roll the ball (with either foot) towards the middle of the goal.

10. The use your left foot to kick the ball at the target on the right side of the goal. Kick the ball before it is closer to the wall than the right and left markers.

11. Finally, run and touch the spot where the ball hit the wall.

12. Give yourself **2 points** if you hit the target. Give yourself **1 more point** if you remembered to touch the spot where the ball hit the wall.

13. Write down your points in **"Today's Scores ."**

14. Do this drill 10 times and count up your points in **"(Part 2)."**

15. Add up your points for **"Today's Score (Part 1)" plus "(Part 2)."** This is your score.

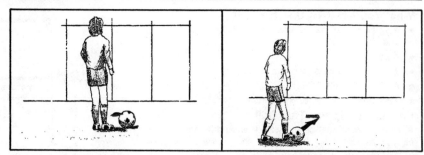

Today's Scores PART 2

YOUR GOAL: A score of 30 or more points

HIT THE TARGET 2 POINTS									
RUN 1 POINT									

	PART 1		PART 2		SCORE
=		+		=	

How To Watch Your Scores Improve

1. Write down your score for today. The first day you do this drill, write your score by **DAY 1**, Write you score for the second day by **DAY 2**, and so on.

2. Did you meet your goal?

NO!

Erase **"Today's Scores"** and do this drill again the next time you **PRACTICE SOCCER BY YOURSELF.**

YES!

WELL DONE! The next time you **PRACTICE SOCCER BY YOURSELF** you can move up to the drill on the next page.

Also cut off the number on the top of this page. Then turn to the **PROGRESS CHART** at the end of the book.

DAY	SCORE
1	
2	
3	
4	
5	
6	
7	
8	
9	
10	

DAY	SCORE
11	
12	
13	
14	
15	
16	
17	
18	
19	
20	

DAY	SCORE
21	
22	
23	
24	
25	
26	
27	
28	
29	
30	

BALL BOUNCING TO MID-GOAL, TURN AROUND SHOT AT THE SIDE

What You Need To Do This Drill

- A small area of flat ground with a wall at one end
- A soccer ball
- 3 markers (rags, paper, cup tops, etc.)
- A piece of chalk
- This page, a pencil and an eraser

How to Set Up For This Drill

A. Draw a small goal on the wall. It should be as high as you can reach and 6 large steps wide.

B. Draw targets at the left and right ends of the goal. Each target should be 2 steps wide and go from the ground to the top of the goal.

C. Place a marker 6 large steps out from the left end of the goal. Place another marker 6 large steps out from the right end of the goal. Place a third marker 8 large steps out from the center of the goal.

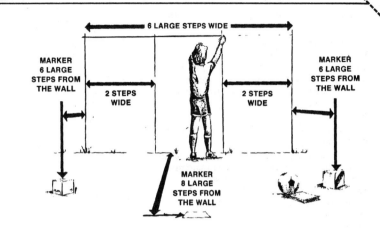

How To Do This Drill

1. Stand with the ball near the center marker. Stand with your back to the goal.

2. Throw the ball gently over your head towards the middle of the goal.

3. Then turn around. Use your right foot to kick the ball at the target on the left side of the goal. Kick the ball before it bounces twice and before it is closer to the wall than the right and left markers.

4. Finally run and touch the spot where the ball hit the wall

5. Give yourself **2 points** if the ball hit the target. Give yourself **1 more point** if you remembered to touch the spot where the ball hit the wall.

6. Write down your points in **"Today's Scores (Part 1)."**

7. Do this drill 10 times and count up your points in **"(Part 1)."**   **GO TO THE NEXT PAGE**

Today's Scores PART 1

HIT THE TARGET 2 POINTS												
RUN 1 POINT												

=

SCORE PART 1

BALL BOUNCING TO MID-GOAL,
TURN AROUND SHOT AT THE SIDE (Continued)

8. Stand with the ball near the center marker. Stand with your back to the goal.

9. Throw the ball gently over your head towards the middle of the goal.

10. Then turn around. Use your left foot to kick the ball at the target on the right side of the goal. Kick the ball before it bounces twice and before it is closer to the wall than the right and left markers.

11. Finally, run and touch the spot where the ball hit the wall.

12. Give yourself **2 points** if you hit the target. Give yourself **1 more point** if you remembered to run immediately and touch the spot where the ball hit the wall.

13. Write down your points in **"Today's Scores (Part 2)."**

14. Do this drill 10 times and count up your points in **"(Part 2)."**

15. Add up your points for **"Today's Score (Part 1)" plus "(Part 2)."** This is your score.

Today's Scores PART 2

HIT THE TARGET 2 POINTS										
RUN 1 POINT										

YOUR GOAL: A score of 30 or more points

PART 1		PART 2		SCORE
=	+		=	

How To Watch Your Scores Improve

1. Write down your score for today. The first day you do this drill, write your score by **DAY 1**, Write you score for the second day by **DAY 2**, and so on.

2. Did you meet your goal?

NO!

Erase **"Today's Scores"** and do this drill again the next time you **PRACTICE SOCCER BY YOURSELF.**

YES!

WELL DONE! The next time you **PRACTICE SOCCER BY YOURSELF** you can move up to the drill on the next page.

Also cut off the number on the top of this page. Then turn to the **PROGRESS CHART** at the end of the book.

DAY	SCORE	DAY	SCORE	DAY	SCORE
1		11		21	
2		12		22	
3		13		23	
4		14		24	
5		15		25	
6		16		26	
7		17		27	
8		18		28	
9		19		29	
10		20		30	

SET SHOT AT THE FAR POST

What You Need To Do This Drill

- A small area of flat ground with a wall at one end
- A soccer ball
- 2 markers (rags, paper, cup tops, etc.)
- A piece of chalk
- This page, a pencil and an eraser

How to Set Up For This Drill

A. Draw a small goal on the wall. It should be as high as you can reach and 6 large steps wide.

B. Draw targets at the left and right ends of the goal. Each target should be 1 step wide and go from the ground to the top of the goal.

C. Place a marker 6 large steps out from the left end of the goal. Place another marker 6 large steps out from the right end of the goal.

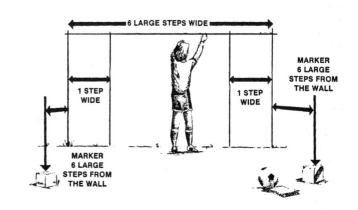

How To Do This Drill

1. Set the ball near the marker on the right side of the goal. Stand facing the goal.

2. Then use your left foot to kick the ball at the target on the left side of the goal.

3. Finally run and touch the spot where the ball hit the wall.

4. Give yourself **2 points** if the ball hit the target. Give yourself **1 more point** if you remembered to touch the spot where the ball hit the wall.

5. Write down your points in **"Today's Scores (Part 1)."**

6. Do this drill 10 times and count up your points in **"(Part 1)."** **GO TO THE NEXT PAGE**

Today's Scores PART 1

HIT THE TARGET 2 POINTS										
RUN I POINT										

SCORE PART 1

=

SET SHOT AT THE FAR POST (Continued)

7. Set the ball near the marker on the left side of the goal. Stand facing the goal.

8. Then use your right foot to kick the ball at the target on the right side of the goal.

9. Finally run and touch the spot where the ball hit the wall.

10. Give yourself **2 points** if you hit the target. Give yourself **1 more point** if you remembered to touch the spot where the ball hit the wall.

11. Write down your points in **"Today's Scores (Part 2)."**

12. . Do this drill 10 times and count up your points in **"(Part 2)."**

13. Add up your points for **"Today's Score (Part 1)" plus "(Part 2)."** This is your score.

Today's Scores PART 2

HIT THE TARGET 2 POINTS										
RUN I POINT										

YOUR GOAL: A score of 30 or more points

PART 1		PART 2		SCORE
=	+		=	

How To Watch Your Scores Improve

1. Write down your score for today. The first day you do this drill, write your score by **DAY 1**, Write you score for the second day by **DAY 2**, and so on.

2. Did you meet your goal?

NO!

Erase **"Today's Scores"** and do this drill again the next time you **PRACTICE SOCCER BY YOURSELF.**

YES!

WELL DONE! The next time you **PRACTICE SOCCER BY YOURSELF** you can move up to the drill on the next page.

Also cut off the number on the top of this page. Then turn to the **PROGRESS CHART** at the end of the book.

DAY	SCORE
1	
2	
3	
4	
5	
6	
7	
8	
9	
10	

DAY	SCORE
11	
12	
13	
14	
15	
16	
17	
18	
19	
20	

DAY	SCORE
21	
22	
23	
24	
25	
26	
27	
28	
29	
30	

BALL ROLLING TO THE FAR POST, SHOT AT THE FAR POST

What You Need To Do This Drill

- A small area of flat ground with a wall at one end
- A soccer ball
- 3 markers (rags, paper, cup tops, etc.)
- A piece of chalk
- This page, a pencil and an eraser

How to Set Up For This Drill

A. Draw a small goal on the wall. It should be as high as you can reach and 6 large steps wide.

B. Draw targets at the left and right ends of the goal. Each target should be 1 steps wide and go from the ground to the top of the goal.

C. Place a marker 8 large steps out from the left end of the goal. Place another marker 8 large steps out from the right end of the goal. Place a third marker 6 large steps out from the center of the goal.

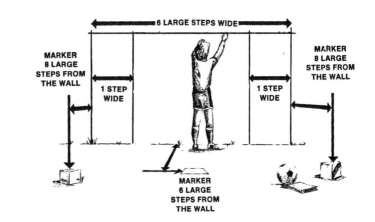

How To Do This Drill

1. Set the ball near the marker on the right side of the goal. Stand facing the goal.

2. Roll the ball (with either foot) toward the left side of the goal.

3. Then use your left foot to kick the ball at the target on the left side of the goal. Kick the ball before it is closer to the wall than the center marker.

4. Finally run and touch the spot where the ball hit the wall

5. Give yourself **2 points** if the ball hit the target. Give yourself **1 more point** if you remembered to touch the spot where the ball hit the wall.

6. Write down your points in **"Today's Scores (Part 1)."**

7. Do this drill 10 times and count up your points in **"(Part 1)."** **GO TO THE NEXT PAGE**

Today's Scores PART 1

HIT THE TARGET 2 POINTS											
RUN 1 POINT											

=

SCORE PART 1

75

BALL ROLLING TO THE FAR POST,
SHOT AT THE FAR POST (Continued)

8. Set the ball near the marker on the left side of the goal. Stand facing the goal.

9. Roll the ball towards the right side of the goal.

10. The use your right foot to kick the ball at the target on the right side of the goal. Kick the ball before it is closer to the wall than the center marker.

11. Finally, run and touch the spot where the ball hit the wall.

12. Give yourself **2 points** if the ball hit the target. Give yourself **1 more point** if you remembered to run and touch the spot where the ball hit the wall.

13. Write down your points in **"Today's Scores (Part 2)."**

14. Do this drill 10 times and count up your points in **"(Part 2)."**

15. Add up your points for **"Today's Score (Part 1)"** plus **"(Part 2)."** This is your score.

Today's Scores PART 2

HIT THE TARGET 2 POINTS										
RUN 1 POINT										

YOUR GOAL: A score of 30 or more points

	PART 1		PART 2		SCORE
=		+		=	

How To Watch Your Scores Improve

1. Write down your score for today. The first day you do this drill, write your score by **DAY 1**, Write you score for the second day by **DAY 2**, and so on.

2. Did you meet your goal?

NO!

Erase **"Today's Scores"** and do this drill again the next time you **PRACTICE SOCCER BY YOURSELF.**

YES!

WELL DONE! The next time you **PRACTICE SOCCER BY YOURSELF** you can move up to the drill on the next page.

Also cut off the number on the top of this page. Then turn to the **PROGRESS CHART** at the end of the book.

DAY	SCORE	DAY	SCORE	DAY	SCORE
1		11		21	
2		12		22	
3		13		23	
4		14		24	
5		15		25	
6		16		26	
7		17		27	
8		18		28	
9		19		29	
10		20		30	

BALL ROLLING TO THE NEAR POST, SHOT AT THE FAR POST

What You Need To Do This Drill

- A small area of flat ground with a wall at one end
- A soccer ball
- 3 markers (rags, paper, cup tops, etc.)
- A piece of chalk
- This page, a pencil and an eraser

How to Set Up For This Drill

A. Draw a small goal on the wall. It should be as high as you can reach and 6 large steps wide.

B. Draw targets at the left and right ends of the goal. Each target should be 1 step wide and go from the ground to the top of the goal.

C. Place a marker 8 large steps out from the left end of the goal. Place another marker 8 large steps out from the right end of the goal. Place a third marker 6 large steps out from the center of the goal.

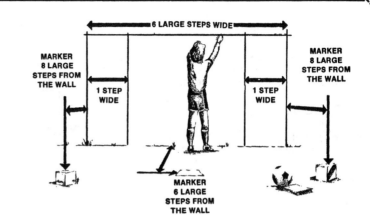

How To Do This Drill

1. Set the ball near the marker on the right side of the goal. Stand facing the goal.

2. Roll the ball (with either foot) toward the right side of the goal.

3. Then use your right foot to kick the ball at the target on the left side of the goal. Kick the ball before it is closer to the wall than the center marker.

4. Finally run and touch the spot where the ball hit the wall

5. Give yourself **2 points** if the ball hit the target. Give yourself **1 more point** if you remembered to run and touch the spot where the ball hit the wall.

6. Write down your points in **"Today's Scores (Part 1)."**

7. Do this drill 10 times and count up your points in **"(Part 1)."**

Today's Scores PART 1

HIT THE TARGET 2 POINTS										
RUN 1 POINT										

SCORE PART 1
=

BALL ROLLING TO THE NEAR POST,
SHOT AT THE FAR POST (Continued)

8. Set the ball near the marker on the left side of the goal. Stand facing the goal.

9. Roll the ball towards the left side of the goal.

10. Then use your left foot to kick the ball at the target on the right side of the goal. Kick the ball before it is closer to the wall than the center marker.

11. Finally, run and touch the spot where the ball hit the wall.

12. Give yourself **2 points** if you hit the target. Give yourself **1 more point** if you remembered to run and touch the spot where the ball hit the wall.

13. Write down your points in **"Today's Scores (Part 2)."**

14. Do this drill 10 times and count up your points in **"(Part 2)."**

15. Add up your points for **"Today's Score (Part 1)" plus "(Part 2)."** This is your score.

Today's Scores PART 2

YOUR GOAL: A score of 30 or more points

HIT THE TARGET 2 POINTS										
RUN 1 POINT										

	PART 1		PART 2		SCORE
=		+		=	

How To Watch Your Scores Improve

1. Write down your score for today. The first day you do this drill, write your score by **DAY 1**, Write you score for the second day by **DAY 2**, and so on.

2. Did you meet your goal?

NO!

Erase **"Today's Scores"** and do this drill again the next time you **PRACTICE SOCCER BY YOURSELF.**

YES!

WELL DONE! The next time you **PRACTICE SOCCER BY YOURSELF** you can move up to the drill on the next page.

Also cut off the number on the top of this page. Then turn to the **PROGRESS CHART** at the end of the book.

DAY	SCORE	DAY	SCORE	DAY	SCORE
1		11		21	
2		12		22	
3		13		23	
4		14		24	
5		15		25	
6		16		26	
7		17		27	
8		18		28	
9		19		29	
10		20		30	

BALL BOUNCING TO THE FAR POST, SHOT AT THE FAR POST

What You Need To Do This Drill

- A small area of flat ground with a wall at one end
- A soccer ball
- 3 markers (rags, paper, cup tops, etc.)
- A piece of chalk
- This page, a pencil and an eraser

How to Set Up For This Drill

A. Draw a small goal on the wall. It should be as high as you can reach and 6 large steps wide.

B. Draw targets at the left and right ends of the goal. Each target should be 1 step wide and go from the ground to the top of the goal.

C. Place a marker 8 large steps out from the left end of the goal. Place another marker 8 large steps out from the right end of the goal. Place a third marker 6 large steps out from the center of the goal.

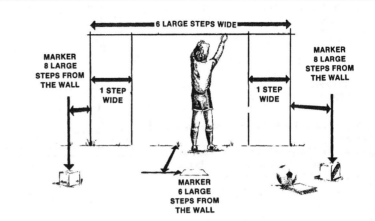

How To Do This Drill

1. Stand with the ball near the marker on the right side of the goal. Stand facing the goal.

2. Bounce the ball towards the left side of the goal.

3. Then use your left foot to kick the ball at the target on the left side of the goal. Kick the ball before it bounces twice and before it is closer to the wall than the center marker

4. Finally run and touch the spot where the ball hit the wall

5. Give yourself **2 points** if the ball hit the target. Give yourself **1 more point** if you remembered to run and touch the spot where the ball hit the wall.

6. Write down your points in **"Today's Scores (Part 1)."**

7. Do this drill 10 times and count up your points in **"(Part 1)."**   **GO TO THE NEXT PAGE**

Today's Scores PART 1

											SCORE PART 1
HIT THE TARGET 2 POINTS											
RUN I POINT											=

BALL BOUNCING TO THE FAR POST,
SHOT AT THE FAR POST (Continued)

8. Stand with the ball near the marker on the left side of the goal. Stand facing the goal.

9. Bounce the ball towards the right side of the goal.

10. Then use your right foot to kick the ball at the target on the right side of the goal. Kick the ball before it bounces twice and before it is closer to the wall than the center marker.

11. Finally, run and touch the spot where the ball hit the wall.

12. Give yourself **2 points** if you hit the target. Give yourself **1 more point** if you remembered to run and touch the spot where the ball hit the wall.

13. Write down your points in **"Today's Scores (Part 2)."**

14. Do this drill 10 times and count up your points in **"(Part 2)."**

15. Add up your points for **"Today's Score (Part 1)"** plus **"(Part 2)."** This is your score.

Today's Scores PART 2

YOUR GOAL: A score of 30 or more points

HIT THE TARGET 2 POINTS										
RUN 1 POINT										

	PART 1		PART 2		SCORE
=		+		=	

How To Watch Your Scores Improve

1. Write down your score for today. The first day you do this drill, write your score by **DAY 1**, Write you score for the second day by **DAY 2**, and so on.

2. Did you meet your goal?

NO!

Erase **"Today's Scores"** and do this drill again the next time you **PRACTICE SOCCER BY YOURSELF.**

YES!

WELL DONE! The next time you **PRACTICE SOCCER BY YOURSELF** you can move up to the drill on the next page.

Also cut off the number on the top of this page. Then turn to the **PROGRESS CHART** at the end of the book.

DAY	SCORE
1	
2	
3	
4	
5	
6	
7	
8	
9	
10	

DAY	SCORE
11	
12	
13	
14	
15	
16	
17	
18	
19	
20	

DAY	SCORE
21	
22	
23	
24	
25	
26	
27	
28	
29	
30	

BALL BOUNCING TO THE NEAR POST, SHOT AT THE FAR POST

What You Need To Do This Drill

- A small area of flat ground with a wall at one end
- A soccer ball
- 3 markers (rags, paper, cup tops, etc.)
- A piece of chalk
- This page, a pencil and an eraser

How to Set Up For This Drill

A. Draw a small goal on the wall. It should be as high as you can reach and 6 large steps wide.

B. Draw targets at the left and right ends of the goal. Each target should be 1 step wide and go from the ground to the top of the goal.

C. Place a marker 8 large steps out from the left end of the goal. Place another marker 8 large steps out from the right end of the goal. Place a third marker 6 large steps out from the center of the goal.

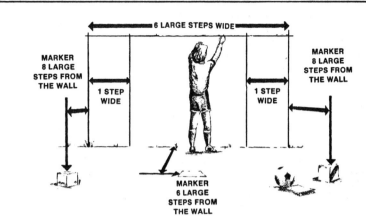

How To Do This Drill

1. Stand with the ball near the marker on the right side of the goal. Stand facing the goal.

2. Bounce the ball towards the right side of the goal.

3. Then use your right foot to kick the ball at the target on the left side of the goal. Kick the ball before it bounces twice and before it is closer to the wall than the center marker

4. Finally run and touch the spot where the ball hit the wall

5. Give yourself **2 points** if the ball hit the target. Give yourself **1 more point** if you remembered to run and touch the spot where the ball hit the wall.

6. Write down your points in **"Today's Scores (Part 1)."**

7. Do this drill 10 times and count up your points in **"(Part 1)."**   **GO TO THE NEXT PAGE**

Today's Scores PART 1

HIT THE TARGET 2 POINTS										
RUN 1 POINT										

SCORE PART 1

=

BALL BOUNCING TO THE NEAR POST, SHOT AT THE FAR POST (Continued)

8. Stand with the ball near the marker on the left side of the goal. Stand facing the goal.

9. Bounce the ball towards the left side of the goal.

10. Then use your left foot to kick the ball at the target on the right side of the goal. Kick the ball before it bounces twice and before it is closer to the wall than the center marker.

11. Finally, run and touch the spot where the ball hit the wall.

12. Give yourself **2 points** if you hit the target. Give yourself **1 more point** if you remembered to run and touch the spot where the ball hit the wall.

13. Write down your points in **"Today's Scores (Part 2)."**

14. Do this drill 10 times and count up your points in **"(Part 2)."**

15. Add up your points for **"Today's Score (Part 1)" plus "(Part 2)."** This is your score.

Today's Scores PART 2

YOUR GOAL: A score of 30 or more points

HIT THE TARGET 2 POINTS										
RUN 1 POINT										

	PART 1		PART 2		SCORE
=		+		=	

How To Watch Your Scores Improve

1. Write down your score for today. The first day you do this drill, write your score by **DAY 1**, Write you score for the second day by **DAY 2**, and so on.

2. Did you meet your goal?

NO!

Erase **"Today's Scores"** and do this drill again the next time you **PRACTICE SOCCER BY YOURSELF.**

YES!

WELL DONE! The next time you **PRACTICE SOCCER BY YOURSELF** you can move up to the drill on the next page.

Also cut off the number on the top of this page. Then turn to the **PROGRESS CHART** at the end of the book.

DAY	SCORE	DAY	SCORE	DAY	SCORE
1		11		21	
2		12		22	
3		13		23	
4		14		24	
5		15		25	
6		16		26	
7		17		27	
8		18		28	
9		19		29	
10		20		30	

BALL BOUNCING TO THE FAR POST, TURN AROUND SHOT AT THE FAR POST

What You Need To Do This Drill

- A small area of flat ground with a wall at one end
- A soccer ball
- 3 markers (rags, paper, cup tops, etc.)
- A piece of chalk
- This page, a pencil and an eraser

How to Set Up For This Drill

A. Draw a small goal on the wall. It should be as high as you can reach and 6 large steps wide.

B. Draw targets at the left and right ends of the goal. Each target should be 1 step wide and go from the ground to the top of the goal.

C. Place a marker 8 large steps out from the left end of the goal. Place another marker 8 large steps out from the right end of the goal. Place a third marker 6 large steps out from the center of the goal.

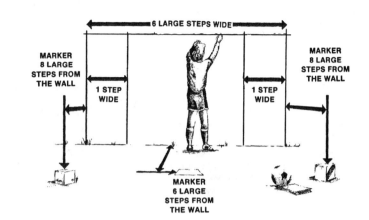

How To Do This Drill

1. Stand with the ball near the marker on the right side of the goal. Stand with your back to the goal.

2. Throw the ball gently over your head towards the left side of the goal.

3. Turn around. Use your left foot to kick the ball at the target on the left side of the goal. Kick the ball before it bounces twice and before it is closer to the wall than the center marker

4. Finally run and touch the spot where the ball hit the wall

5. Give yourself **2 points** if the ball hit the target. Give yourself **1 more point** if you remembered to run and touch the spot where the ball hit the wall.

6. Write down your points in **"Today's Scores (Part 1)."**

7. Do this drill 10 times and count up your points in **"(Part 1)."**   **GO TO THE NEXT PAGE**

Today's Scores PART 1

												SCORE PART 1
HIT THE TARGET 2 POINTS											=	
RUN I POINT												

BALL BOUNCING TO THE FAR POST, TURN AROUND SHOT AT THE FAR POST (Continued)

8. Stand with the ball near the marker on the left side of the goal. Stand with your back to the goal.

9. Throw the ball gently over your head towards the right side of the goal.

10. Turn around. Use your right foot to kick the ball at the target on the right side of the goal. Kick the ball before it bounces twice and before it is closer to the wall than the center marker.

11. Finally, run and touch the spot where the ball hit the wall.

12. Give yourself **2 points** if you hit the target. Give yourself **1 more point** if you remembered to run and touch the spot where the ball hit the wall.

13. Write down your points in **"Today's Scores (Part 2)."**

14. Do this drill 10 times and count up your points in **"(Part 2)."**

15. Add up your points for **"Today's Score (Part 1)" plus "(Part 2)."** This is your score.

Today's Scores   PART 2

YOUR GOAL: A score of 30 or more points

HIT THE TARGET 2 POINTS									
RUN I POINT									

	PART 1		PART 2		SCORE
=		+		=	

How To Watch Your Scores Improve

1. Write down your score for today. The first day you do this drill, write your score by **DAY 1**, Write you score for the second day by **DAY 2**, and so on.

2. Did you meet your goal?

NO!

Erase **"Today's Scores"** and do this drill again the next time you **PRACTICE SOCCER BY YOURSELF.**

YES!

WELL DONE! The next time you **PRACTICE SOCCER BY YOURSELF** you can move up to the drill on the next page.

Also cut off the number on the top of this page. Then turn to the **PROGRESS CHART** at the end of the book.

DAY	SCORE
1	
2	
3	
4	
5	
6	
7	
8	
9	
10	

DAY	SCORE
11	
12	
13	
14	
15	
16	
17	
18	
19	
20	

DAY	SCORE
21	
22	
23	
24	
25	
26	
27	
28	
29	
30	

BALL BOUNCING TO THE NEAR POST, TURN AROUND SHOT AT THE FAR POST

What You Need To Do This Drill

- A small area of flat ground with a wall at one end
- A soccer ball
- 3 markers (rags, paper, cup tops, etc.)
- A piece of chalk
- This page, a pencil and an eraser

How to Set Up For This Drill

A. Draw a small goal on the wall. It should be as high as you can reach and 6 large steps wide.

B. Draw targets at the left and right ends of the goal. Each target should be 1 step wide and go from the ground to the top of the goal.

C. Place a marker 8 large steps out from the left end of the goal. Place another marker 8 large steps out from the right end of the goal. Place a third marker 6 large steps out from the center of the goal.

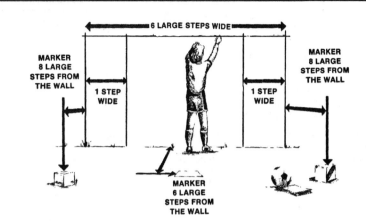

6 LARGE STEPS WIDE

MARKER 8 LARGE STEPS FROM THE WALL

1 STEP WIDE

MARKER 8 LARGE STEPS FROM THE WALL

1 STEP WIDE

MARKER 6 LARGE STEPS FROM THE WALL

How To Do This Drill

1. Stand with the ball near the marker on the right side of the goal. Stand with your back to the goal.

2. Throw the ball gently over your head towards the right side of the goal.

3. Then turn around. Use your right foot to kick the ball at the target on the left side of the goal. Kick the ball before it bounces twice and before it is closer to the wall than the center marker

4. Finally run and touch the spot where the ball hit the wall

5. Give yourself **2 points** if the ball hit the target. Give yourself **1 more point** if you remembered to run and touch the spot where the ball hit the wall.

6. Write down your points in **"Today's Scores (Part 1)."**

7. Do this drill 10 times and count up your points in **"(Part 1)."**   **GO TO THE NEXT PAGE**

Today's Scores PART 1

HIT THE TARGET 2 POINTS											
RUN 1 POINT											

SCORE PART 1

=

BALL BOUNCING TO THE NEAR POST,
TURN AROUND SHOT AT THE FAR POST (Continued)

8. Stand with the ball near the marker on the left side of the goal. Stand with your back to the goal.

9. Throw the ball gently over your head towards the left side of the goal.

10. Then turn around. Use your left foot to kick the ball at the target on the right side of the goal. Kick the ball before it bounces twice and before it is closer to the wall than the center marker.

11. Finally, run and touch the spot where the ball hit the wall.

12. Give yourself **2 points** if you hit the target. Give yourself **1 more point** if you remembered to run and touch the spot where the ball hit the wall.

13. Write down your points in **"Today's Scores (Part 2)."**

14. Do this drill 10 times and count up your points in **"(Part 2)."**

15. Add up your points for **"Today's Score (Part 1)"** plus **"(Part 2)."** This is your score.

Today's Scores   PART 2

YOUR GOAL: A score of 30 or more points

HIT THE TARGET 2 POINTS											
RUN 1 POINT											

	PART 1		PART 2		SCORE
=		+		=	

How To Watch Your Scores Improve

1. Write down your score for today. The first day you do this drill, write your score by **DAY 1**, Write you score for the second day by **DAY 2**, and so on.

2. Did you meet your goal?

NO!

Erase **"Today's Scores"** and do this drill again the next time you **PRACTICE SOCCER BY YOURSELF.**

YES!

WELL DONE! The next time you **PRACTICE SOCCER BY YOURSELF** you can move up to the drill on the next page.

Also cut off the number on the top of this page. Then turn to the **PROGRESS CHART** at the end of the book.

DAY	SCORE	DAY	SCORE	DAY	SCORE
1		11		21	
2		12		22	
3		13		23	
4		14		24	
5		15		25	
6		16		26	
7		17		27	
8		18		28	
9		19		29	
10		20		30	

HEAD SHOOTING LOW

What You Need To Do This Drill
- A small area of flat ground with a wall at one end
- A soccer ball
- 1 marker (rag, paper, cup tops, etc.)
- A piece of chalk
- This page, a pencil and an eraser

How to Set Up For This Drill
A. Draw a small goal on the wall. It should be as high as you can reach and 6 large steps wide.

B. Draw targets at the left and right ends of the goal. Each target should be 2 steps wide and go from the ground to your knee.

C. Place a marker 3 large steps out from the center of the goal.

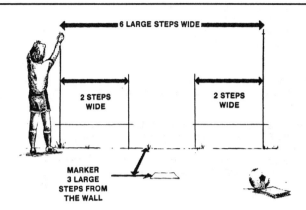

6 LARGE STEPS WIDE

2 STEPS WIDE

2 STEPS WIDE

MARKER 3 LARGE STEPS FROM THE WALL

How To Do This Drill

1. Stand with the ball on the side of, and behind the center marker. Do steps 1-6 10 times from the right side of the center marker and 10 times from the left.

2. Throw the ball high up on the wall, straight in front of you.

3. When the ball bounces off the wall, head the ball towards the target on the left. Hit the ball only once.

4. Finally run and touch the spot where the ball hit the wall.

5. Give yourself **2 points** if the ball hit the target. Give yourself **1 more point** if you remembered to touch the spot where the ball hit the wall.

6. Write down your points in **"Today's Scores (Part 1)."**

7. Do steps 1-6 20 times. Ten times starting from the right side of the center marker and heading at the left target. Ten times from the left side of the center marker and heading the right target.

8. Add up your points in **"Today's Scores."** This is your score.

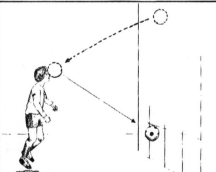

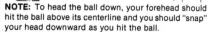

NOTE: To head the ball down, your forehead should hit the ball above its centerline and you should "snap" your head downward as you hit the ball.

NOTE: When you hit the ball with your head:

a. be sure to hit the ball with the top of your forehead. Hitting ther ball with the your head won't hurt if you use your forehead.

b. keep your eyes open and watch the ball as your head hits it.

c. keep your mouth closed.

d. swing your body from the waist to get good power.

YOUR GOAL: A score of 30 or more points

Today's Scores

	1	2	3	4	5	6	7	8	9	10	11	12	13	14	15	16	17	18	19	20	TOTAL
HIT THE TARGET 2 POINTS																					
RUN 1 POINT																					

How To Watch Your Score Improve

1. Write down your score for today. The first day you do this drill, write your score by **DAY 1**, Write you score for the second day by **DAY 2**, and so on.

2. Did you meet your goal?

NO!

Erase **"Today's Scores"** and do this drill again the next time you **PRACTICE SOCCER BY YOURSELF.**

YES!

WELL DONE! The next time you **PRACTICE SOCCER BY YOURSELF** you can move up to the drill on the next page.

Also cut off the number on the top of this page. Then turn to the **PROGRESS CHART** at the end of the book.

DAY	SCORE
1	
2	
3	
4	
5	
6	
7	
8	
9	
10	

DAY	SCORE
11	
12	
13	
14	
15	
16	
17	
18	
19	
20	

DAY	SCORE
21	
22	
23	
24	
25	
26	
27	
28	
29	
30	

NOTES:

BALL ROLLING TO MID-GOAL, SHOT AT THE POST

What You Need To Do This Drill

- A small area of flat ground with a wall at one end
- A soccer ball
- 3 markers (rags, paper, cup tops, etc.)
- A piece of chalk
- This page, a pencil and an eraser

How to Set Up For This Drill

A. Draw a small goal on the wall. It should be as high as you can reach and 6 large steps wide.

B. Draw targets at the left and right ends of the goal. Each target should be 1 steps wide and go from the ground to the top of the goal.

C. Place a marker 6 large steps out from the left end of the goal. Place another marker 6 large steps out from the right end of the goal. Place a third marker 8 large steps out from the center of the goal.

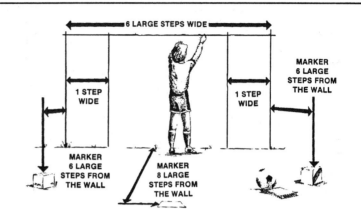

6 LARGE STEPS WIDE

1 STEP WIDE

1 STEP WIDE

MARKER 6 LARGE STEPS FROM THE WALL

MARKER 6 LARGE STEPS FROM THE WALL

MARKER 8 LARGE STEPS FROM THE WALL

How To Do This Drill

1. Set the ball near the center marker. Stand facing the goal.

2. Roll the ball (with either foot) toward the middle of the goal.

3. Then use your right foot to kick the ball at the target on the left side of the goal. Kick the ball before it is closer to the wall than the right and left markers.

4. Finally run and touch the spot where the ball hit the wall

5. Give yourself **2 points** if the ball hit the target. Give yourself **1 more point** if you remembered to touch the spot where the ball hit the wall.

6. Write down your points in **"Today's Scores (Part 1)."**

7. Do this drill 10 times and count up your points in **"(Part 1)."**   **GO TO THE NEXT PAGE**

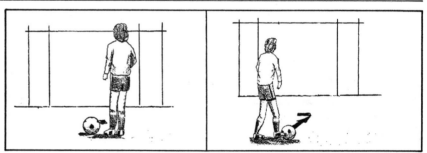

Today's Scores PART 1

HIT THE TARGET 2 POINTS											
RUN 1 POINT											

SCORE PART 1

=

BALL ROLLING TO MID-GOAL, SHOT AT THE POST (Continued)

8. Set the ball near the center marker. Stand facing the goal.

9. Roll the ball (with either foot) towards the middle of the goal.

10. The use your left foot to kick the ball at the target on the right side of the goal. Kick the ball before it is closer to the wall than the left and right markers.

11. Finally, run and touch the spot where the ball hit the wall.

12. Give yourself **2 points** if the ball hit the target. Give yourself **1 more point** if you remembered to run and touch the spot where the ball hit the wall.

13. Write down your points in **"Today's Scores (Part 2)."**

14. Do this drill 10 times and count up your points in **"(Part 2)."**

15. Add up your points for **"Today's Scores (Part 1)" plus "(Part 2)."** This is your score.

Today's Scores   PART 2

YOUR GOAL: A score of 30 or more points

HIT THE TARGET 2 POINTS										
RUN 1 POINT										

	PART 1		PART 2		SCORE
=		+		=	

How To Watch Your Scores Improve

1. Write down your score for today. The first day you do this drill, write your score by **DAY 1**, Write you score for the second day by **DAY 2**, and so on.

2. Did you meet your goal?

NO!

Erase **"Today's Scores"** and do this drill again the next time you **PRACTICE SOCCER BY YOURSELF.**

YES!

WELL DONE! The next time you **PRACTICE SOCCER BY YOURSELF** you can move up to the drill on the next page.

Also cut off the number on the top of this page. Then turn to the **PROGRESS CHART** at the end of the book.

DAY	SCORE	DAY	SCORE	DAY	SCORE
1		11		21	
2		12		22	
3		13		23	
4		14		24	
5		15		25	
6		16		26	
7		17		27	
8		18		28	
9		19		29	
10		20		30	

BALL BOUNCING TO MID-GOAL, TURN AROUND SHOT AT THE POST

What You Need To Do This Drill

- A small area of flat ground with a wall at one end
- A soccer ball
- 3 markers (rags, paper, cup tops, etc.)
- A piece of chalk
- This page, a pencil and an eraser

How to Set Up For This Drill

A. Draw a small goal on the wall. It should be as high as you can reach and 6 large steps wide.

B. Draw targets at the left and right ends of the goal. Each target should be 1 step wide and go from the ground to the top of the goal.

C. Place a marker 6 large steps out from the left end of the goal. Place another marker 6 large steps out from the right end of the goal. Place a third marker 8 large steps out from the center of the goal.

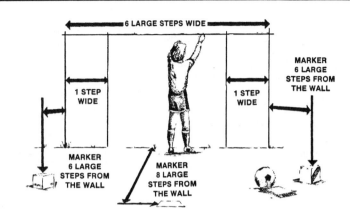

6 LARGE STEPS WIDE

1 STEP WIDE

1 STEP WIDE

MARKER 6 LARGE STEPS FROM THE WALL

MARKER 6 LARGE STEPS FROM THE WALL

MARKER 8 LARGE STEPS FROM THE WALL

How To Do This Drill

1. Stand with the ball near the center marker. Stand with your back to the goal.

2. Throw the ball gently over your head towards the middle of the goal.

3. Turn around. Use your right foot to kick the ball at the target on the left side of the goal. Kick the ball before it bounces twice and before it is closer to the wall than the right and left markers.

4. Finally run and touch the spot where the ball hit the wall

5. Give yourself **2 points** if the ball hit the target. Give yourself **1 more point** if you remembered to run and touch the spot where the ball hit the wall.

6. Write down your points in **"Today's Scores (Part 1)."**

7. Do this drill 10 times and count up your points in **"(Part 1)."**　　**GO TO THE NEXT PAGE**

Today's Scores PART 1

												SCORE PART 1
HIT THE TARGET 2 POINTS												
RUN 1 POINT											=	

91

BALL BOUNCING TO MID-GOAL, TURN AROUND SHOT AT THE POST (Continued)

8. Stand with the ball near the center marker. Stand with your back to the goal.

9. Throw the ball gently over your head towards the middle of the goal.

10. Turn around. Use your left foot to kick the ball at the target on the right side of the goal. Kick the ball before it bounces twice and before it is closer to the wall than the right and left markers.

11. Finally, run and touch the spot where the ball hit the wall.

12. Give yourself **2 points** if you hit the target. Give yourself **1 more point** if you remembered to run and touch the spot where the ball hit the wall.

13. Write down your points in **"Today's Scores (Part 2)."**

14. Do this drill 10 times and count up your points in **"(Part 2)."**

15. Add up your points for **"Today's Score (Part 1)"** plus **"(Part 2)."** This is your score.

Today's Scores   PART 2

HIT THE TARGET 2 POINTS										
RUN 1 POINT										

YOUR GOAL: A score of 30 or more points

	PART 1		PART 2		SCORE
=		+		=	

How To Watch Your Scores Improve

1. Write down your score for today. The first day you do this drill, write your score by **DAY 1**, Write you score for the second day by **DAY 2**, and so on.

2. Did you meet your goal?

NO!

Erase **"Today's Scores"** and do this drill again the next time you **PRACTICE SOCCER BY YOURSELF.**

YES!

WELL DONE! The next time you **PRACTICE SOCCER BY YOURSELF** you can move up to the drill on the next page.

Also cut off the number on the top of this page. Then turn to the **PROGRESS CHART** at the end of the book.

DAY	SCORE	DAY	SCORE	DAY	SCORE
1		11		21	
2		12		22	
3		13		23	
4		14		24	
5		15		25	
6		16		26	
7		17		27	
8		18		28	
9		19		29	
10		20		30	

Why Should You Practice...

. . .JUGGLING?

Picture yourself in a soccer game. You are near the other team's goal.

The ball comes to you from one of your midfielders so your back is to their goal.

Now, think about what you might do. . .

You could stop the ball and pass it to a teammate. This might be a good move.

You could stop the ball, flick the ball to the side, turn and shoot — this would be a great move.

You are open for a shot and if you get it off quickly you could score.

Fortunately, you have been practicing your juggling, so you know how to move the ball to the side so you can shoot.

Ball juggling helps you learn how to move the ball around you, from one leg to the other; from your head to your feet; from one side to the other. You will learn how to control the ball with the tops of both feet, your thighs, and your head.

ONE-BOUNCE JUGGLE

What You Need To Do This Drill
- A small area of flat ground
- A soccer ball
- This page, a pencil and an eraser

How To Set Up For This Drill
A. No set up is needed.

How To Do This Drill
1. Hold the ball in front of you.

2. Throw the ball up in the air and let it bounce once.

3. Before the ball bounces twice, hit it gently back into the air. You can use your feet, legs body or head.

4. Let the ball bounce again and hit it gently back into the air.

5. Continue to let the ball bounce once and then hit it back into the air.
Bounce ---- Hit ---- Bounce ---- Hit ---- Bounce ---- Hit ----

6. Do this as many times as you can.

7. Count how many times you hit the ball before it bounces more than once. This is your score.

8. When the ball bounces more than once: stop the drill; write down your score in **"Today's Scores"**; and start the drill at step 1.

9. Do this drill for five minutes.

NOTE: When you juggle the ball correctly, it will not spin at all or it may backspin. No spin or a slow backspin will help keep the ball close to you.
NOTE: Watch the ball closely at all times.

Today's Scores

YOUR GOAL: A score of 6 or more hits in a row

HITS																						

How To Watch Your Score Improve

1. Write down your score for today. The first day you do this drill, write your score by **DAY 1**, Write you score for the second day by **DAY 2**, and so on.

2. Did you meet your goal?

NO!

Erase **"Today's Scores"** and do this drill again the next time you **PRACTICE SOCCER BY YOURSELF.**

YES!

WELL DONE! The next time you **PRACTICE SOCCER BY YOURSELF** you can move up to the drill on the next page.

Also cut off the number on the top of this page. Then turn to the **PROGRESS CHART** at the end of the book.

DAY	SCORE
1	
2	
3	
4	
5	
6	
7	
8	
9	
10	

DAY	SCORE
11	
12	
13	
14	
15	
16	
17	
18	
19	
20	

DAY	SCORE
21	
22	
23	
24	
25	
26	
27	
28	
29	
30	

NOTES:

ONE-BOUNCE JUGGLES — ALTERNATING SIDES

What You Need To Do This Drill
- A small area of flat ground
- A soccer ball
- This page, a pencil and an eraser

How To Set Up For This Drill
A. No set up is needed.

How To Do This Drill
1. Hold the ball in front of you.

2. Throw the ball up in the air and let it bounce once.

3. One-bounce juggle. Change (alternate) side that touch the ball.
Ball bounces ---- hit it with your right leg or foot ---- ball bounces ---- hit it with your left leg or foot ---- ball bounces ---- hit it with your right leg or foot ---- ball bounces ---- hit it with your left leg or foot ---- (as many times as you can)

4. Count how many times you hit the ball before it bounces more than once. This is your score.

5. When the ball bounces more than once: stop the drill; write down your score in **"Today's Scores"**; and start the drill at step 1.

6. Do this drill for five minutes.

Ball bounces...   And falls to the right foot...

Right foot kick...   Ball bounces...   And falls to the left foot...

Left foot kick...   Ball bounces... And falls to the right foot...

Today's Scores

YOUR GOAL: A score of 6 or more hits in a row

HITS																			

How To Watch Your Score Improve

1. Write down your score for today. The first day you do this drill, write your score by **DAY 1**, Write you score for the second day by **DAY 2**, and so on.

2. Did you meet your goal?

NO!

Erase **"Today's Scores"** and do this drill again the next time you **PRACTICE SOCCER BY YOURSELF.**

YES!

WELL DONE! The next time you **PRACTICE SOCCER BY YOURSELF** you can move up to the drill on the next page.

Also cut off the number on the top of this page. Then turn to the **PROGRESS CHART** at the end of the book.

DAY	SCORE		DAY	SCORE		DAY	SCORE
1			11			21	
2			12			22	
3			13			23	
4			14			24	
5			15			25	
6			16			26	
7			17			27	
8			18			28	
9			19			29	
10			20			30	

NOTES:

NO-BOUNCE JUGGLES

What You Need To Do This Drill

- A small area of flat ground
- A soccer ball
- This page, a pencil and an eraser

How To Set Up For This Drill

A. No set up is needed.

How To Do This Drill

1. Hold the ball in front of you.

2. Throw the ball up in the air.

3. Before the ball touches the ground, hit it gently back into the air. You can use your feet, legs body or head to hit the ball.

4. As the ball is dropping and before it touches the ground, hit it gently back into the air.

5. Without letting the ball touch the ground, continue to hit it into the air as many times as you can.

6. Count how many times you hit the ball before it touches the ground. This is your score.

8. When the ball hits the ground: stop the drill; write down your score in **"Today's Scores"**; and start the drill at step 1.

9. Do this drill for five minutes.

NOTE: Watch the ball closely at all times.

NOTE: When you juggle the ball correctly, it will not spin at all or it may backspin. No spin or a slow backspin will help keep the ball close to you.

Today's Scores

YOUR GOAL: A score of 6 or more hits in a row

HITS																				

How To Watch Your Score Improve

1. Write down your score for today. The first day you do this drill, write your score by **DAY 1**, Write you score for the second day by **DAY 2**, and so on.

2. Did you meet your goal?

NO!

Erase **"Today's Scores"** and do this drill again the next time you **PRACTICE SOCCER BY YOURSELF.**

YES!

WELL DONE! The next time you **PRACTICE SOCCER BY YOURSELF** you can move up to the drill on the next page.

Also cut off the number on the top of this page. Then turn to the **PROGRESS CHART** at the end of the book.

DAY	SCORE	DAY	SCORE	DAY	SCORE
1		11		21	
2		12		22	
3		13		23	
4		14		24	
5		15		25	
6		16		26	
7		17		27	
8		18		28	
9		19		29	
10		20		30	

NOTES:

NO-BOUNCE JUGGLES — ALTERNATING SIDES

What You Need To Do This Drill
- A small area of flat ground
- A soccer ball
- This page, a pencil and an eraser

How To Set Up For This Drill
A. No set up is needed.

How To Do This Drill

1. Hold the ball in front of you.

2. Throw the ball up in the air.

3. No-bounce juggle. Change (alternate) sides that hit the ball.
Hit the ball with your right leg or foot ---- (no bounce) ---- hit the ball with your left leg or foot ---- (no bounce) ---- hit the ball with your right leg or foot ---- (no bounce) ---- hit the ball with your left leg or foot ---- (no bounce) ----(as many times as you can)

4. Count how many times you hit the ball before it touches the ground. This is your score.

5. When the ball hits the ground: stop the drill; write down your score in **"Today's Scores"**; and start the drill at step 1.

9. Do this drill for five minutes.

NOTE: When you juggle the ball correctly, it will not spin at all or it may backspin. No spin or a slow backspin will help keep the ball close to you.

NOTE: Watch the ball closely at all times.

Today's Scores

YOUR GOAL: A score of 4 or more hits in a row

HITS																				

How To Watch Your Score Improve

1. Write down your score for today. The first day you do this drill, write your score by **DAY 1**, Write you score for the second day by **DAY 2**, and so on.

2. Did you meet your goal?

NO!

Erase **"Today's Scores"** and do this drill again the next time you **PRACTICE SOCCER BY YOURSELF.**

YES!

WELL DONE! The next time you **PRACTICE SOCCER BY YOURSELF** you can move up to the drill on the next page.

Also cut off the number on the top of this page. Then turn to the **PROGRESS CHART** at the end of the book.

DAY	SCORE
1	
2	
3	
4	
5	
6	
7	
8	
9	
10	

DAY	SCORE
11	
12	
13	
14	
15	
16	
17	
18	
19	
20	

DAY	SCORE
21	
22	
23	
24	
25	
26	
27	
28	
29	
30	

NOTES:

NO-BOUNCE JUGGLES — FEET ONLY

What You Need To Do This Drill
- A small area of flat ground
- A soccer ball
- This page, a pencil and an eraser

How To Set Up For This Drill
A. No set up is needed.

How To Do This Drill
1. Throw the ball up in the air.

2. No-bounce juggle the ball using your feet only to touch the ball. (no thighs, body or head).

3. Count how many times you hit the ball before it touches the ground. This is your score.

4. When the ball hits the ground: stop the drill; write down your score in **"Today's Scores"**; and start the drill again at step 1.

5. Do this drill for 5 minutes.

NOTE: Watch the ball closely at all times.

Today's Scores

YOUR GOAL: A score of 8 or more hits in a row

HITS																		

How To Watch Your Score Improve

1. Write down your score for today. The first day you do this drill, write your score by **DAY 1**, Write you score for the second day by **DAY 2**, and so on.

2. Did you meet your goal?

NO!

Erase **"Today's Scores"** and do this drill again the next time you **PRACTICE SOCCER BY YOURSELF.**

YES!

WELL DONE! The next time you **PRACTICE SOCCER BY YOURSELF** you can move up to the drill on the next page.

Also cut off the number on the top of this page. Then turn to the **PROGRESS CHART** at the end of the book.

DAY	SCORE		DAY	SCORE		DAY	SCORE
1			11			21	
2			12			22	
3			13			23	
4			14			24	
5			15			25	
6			16			26	
7			17			27	
8			18			28	
9			19			29	
10			20			30	

NOTES:

HEAD JUGGLING

What You Need To Do This Drill
- A small area of flat ground
- A soccer ball
- This page, a pencil and an eraser

How To Set Up For This Drill
A. No set up is needed.

How To Do This Drill

1. Hold the ball over your head and look up so you can see it. Bend backwards, a little, at the knees.

2. Drop the ball.

3. As the ball falls, straighten up your body so you hit the ball with the top of your forehead.

4. As the ball bounces off your head, bend your body slightly at the knees.

5. As the ball falls, straighten up your body so you hit the ball with the top of you forehead.

6. Head the ball as many times as you can before it falls to the ground.

7. Count how many times you head the ball before it falls to the ground. This is your score.

8. When the ball hits the ground: stop the drill; write down your score in **"Today's Scores"**; start the drill again at step 1.

9. Do this drill for 5 minutes.

NOTE: When you hit the ball with your head;

a. be sure to hit the ball with the top of your forehead. Hitting the ball with your head won't hurt you if you use your forehead.

b. keep your eyes open and watch the ball as your head hits it.

c. keep your mouth shut.

d. swing your body from the waist to get good power.

Today's Scores

YOUR GOAL: A score of 3 or more hits

	1	2	3	4	5	6	7	8	9	10	11	12	13	14	15	16	17	18	19	20
HEADS																				

How To Watch Your Score Improve

1. Write down your score for today. The first day you do this drill, write your score by **DAY 1**, Write you score for the second day by **DAY 2**, and so on.

2. Did you meet your goal?

NO!

Erase **"Today's Scores"** and do this drill again the next time you **PRACTICE SOCCER BY YOURSELF.**

YES!

WELL DONE! The next time you **PRACTICE SOCCER BY YOURSELF** you can move up to the drill on the next page.

Also cut off the number on the top of this page. Then turn to the **PROGRESS CHART** at the end of the book.

DAY	SCORE
1	
2	
3	
4	
5	
6	
7	
8	
9	
10	

DAY	SCORE
11	
12	
13	
14	
15	
16	
17	
18	
19	
20	

DAY	SCORE
21	
22	
23	
24	
25	
26	
27	
28	
29	
30	

NOTES:

ONE-BOUNCE JUGGLES — LIFT START

What You Need To Do This Drill

- A small area of flat ground
- A soccer ball
- This page, a pencil and an eraser

How To Set Up For This Drill

A. No set up is needed.

How To Do This Drill

1. Stand with the ball at your feet.

2. Lift the ball off the ground with your foot and let it bounce.

3. One-bounce juggle the ball. You may hit the ball with either leg or foot, or your body or head.

4. Count how many times you hit the ball before it bounces more than once. This is your score.

5. When the ball hits the ground more than once: stop the drill; write down your score in **"Today's Scores"**; and start the drill again at step 1.

6. Do this drill for 5 minutes.

Pull the Ball Towards You

Let the Ball Spin Up On Your Foot

Kick the Ball Up In the Air

NOTE: It may take you many tries before you can lift the ball with your foot. Don't give up!

Today's Scores

YOUR GOAL: A score of 12 or more hits in a row

HITS																	

How To Watch Your Score Improve

1. Write down your score for today. The first day you do this drill, write your score by **DAY 1**, Write you score for the second day by **DAY 2**, and so on.

2. Did you meet your goal?

NO!

Erase **"Today's Scores"** and do this drill again the next time you **PRACTICE SOCCER BY YOURSELF.**

YES!

WELL DONE! The next time you **PRACTICE SOCCER BY YOURSELF** you can move up to the drill on the next page.

Also cut off the number on the top of this page. Then turn to the **PROGRESS CHART** at the end of the book.

DAY	SCORE	DAY	SCORE	DAY	SCORE
1		11		21	
2		12		22	
3		13		23	
4		14		24	
5		15		25	
6		16		26	
7		17		27	
8		18		28	
9		19		29	
10		20		30	

NOTES:

NO-BOUNCE JUGGLES — LIFT START

What You Need To Do This Drill
- A small area of flat ground
- A soccer ball
- This page, a pencil and an eraser

How To Set Up For This Drill
A. No set up is needed.

How To Do This Drill

1. Stand with the ball at your feet.

2. Lift the ball off the ground with your foot.

3. No-bounce juggle the ball. You may hit the ball with either leg or foot, or your body or head.

4. Count how many times you hit the ball before it touches the ground. This is your score.

5. When the ball touches the ground: stop the drill; write down your score in **"Today's Scores"**; and start the drill again at step 1.

6. Do this drill for 5 minutes.

NOTE: It may take you many tries before you can lift the ball with your foot. Don't give up!

Today's Scores

YOUR GOAL: A score of 8 or more hits in a row

HITS																			

How To Watch Your Score Improve

1. Write down your score for today. The first day you do this drill, write your score by **DAY 1**, Write you score for the second day by **DAY 2**, and so on.

2. Did you meet your goal?

NO!

Erase **"Today's Scores"** and do this drill again the next time you **PRACTICE SOCCER BY YOURSELF.**

YES!

WELL DONE! The next time you **PRACTICE SOCCER BY YOURSELF** you can move up to the drill on the next page.

Also cut off the number on the top of this page. Then turn to the **PROGRESS CHART** at the end of the book.

DAY	SCORE	DAY	SCORE	DAY	SCORE
1		11		21	
2		12		22	
3		13		23	
4		14		24	
5		15		25	
6		16		26	
7		17		27	
8		18		28	
9		19		29	
10		20		30	

NOTES:

HEAD JUGGLING — LIFT START

What You Need To Do This Drill
- A small area of flat ground
- A soccer ball
- This page, a pencil and an eraser

How To Set Up For This Drill
A. No set up is needed.

How To Do This Drill
1. Stand with the ball at your feet.

2. Lift the ball off the ground with your foot and kick the ball straight up, higher than your head.

3. As the ball falls, head it into the air.

4. Head it as many times as you can before it falls to the ground.

5. Count how many times you head the ball. This is your score.

When the ball touches the ground: stop the drill; write down your score in **"Today's Scores"**; start again at **step 1.**

6. Do this drill for 5 minutes.

NOTE: When you hit the ball with your head;

a. be sure to hit the ball with the top of your forehead. Hitting the ball with your head won't hurt you if you use your forehead.

b. keep your eyes open and watch the ball as your head hits it.

c. keep your mouth shut.

d. swing your body from the waist to get good power.

Today's Scores

YOUR GOAL: A score of 4 or more hits

	1	2	3	4	5	6	7	8	9	10	11	12	13	14	15	16	17	18	19	20
NUMBER OF HITS																				

How To Watch Your Score Improve

1. Write down your score for today. The first day you do this drill, write your score by **DAY 1**, Write you score for the second day by **DAY 2**, and so on.

2. Did you meet your goal?

NO!

Erase **"Today's Scores"** and do this drill again the next time you **PRACTICE SOCCER BY YOURSELF.**

YES!

WELL DONE! The next time you **PRACTICE SOCCER BY YOURSELF** you can move up to the drill on the next page.

Also cut off the number on the top of this page. Then turn to the **PROGRESS CHART** at the end of the book.

DAY	SCORE
1	
2	
3	
4	
5	
6	
7	
8	
9	
10	

DAY	SCORE
11	
12	
13	
14	
15	
16	
17	
18	
19	
20	

DAY	SCORE
21	
22	
23	
24	
25	
26	
27	
28	
29	
30	

NOTES:

ONE-BOUNCE JUGGLES TO THE RIGHT

What You Need To Do This Drill
- A small area of flat ground
- A soccer ball
- This page, a pencil and an eraser

How To Set Up For This Drill
A. No set up is needed.

How To Do This Drill

1. Stand with the ball at your feet.

2. Lift the ball off the ground with your foot and let it bounce once.

3. One-bounce juggle the ball using your right foot or leg only. Each time you hit the ball, turn it towards your right side. (See note below)

4. Count how many times in a row you hit the ball to the right before it bounces more than once. This is your score.

5. When the ball doesn't turn to the right or bounces more than once: stop the drill; write down your score in **"Today's Scores"**; and start the drill again at step 1.

6. Do this drill for 5 minutes.

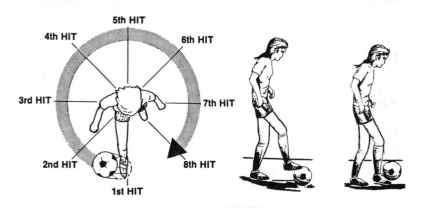

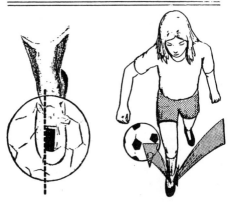

NOTE: To turn the ball to the right, hit the ball a little to the left of its midline.

Today's Scores

YOUR GOAL: A score of 10 or more hits in a row

HITS																			

How To Watch Your Score Improve

1. Write down your score for today. The first day you do this drill, write your score by **DAY 1**, Write you score for the second day by **DAY 2**, and so on.

2. Did you meet your goal?

NO!

Erase **"Today's Scores"** and do this drill again the next time you **PRACTICE SOCCER BY YOURSELF.**

YES!

WELL DONE! The next time you **PRACTICE SOCCER BY YOURSELF** you can move up to the drill on the next page.

Also cut off the number on the top of this page. Then turn to the **PROGRESS CHART** at the end of the book.

DAY	SCORE	DAY	SCORE	DAY	SCORE
1		11		21	
2		12		22	
3		13		23	
4		14		24	
5		15		25	
6		16		26	
7		17		27	
8		18		28	
9		19		29	
10		20		30	

NOTES:

ONE-BOUNCE JUGGLES TO THE LEFT

What You Need To Do This Drill
- A small area of flat ground
- A soccer ball
- This page, a pencil and an eraser

How To Set Up For This Drill
A. No set up is needed.

How To Do This Drill

1. Stand with the ball at your feet.

2. Lift the ball off the ground with your foot and let it bounce once.

3. One-bounce juggle using your left foot or leg only. Each time you hit the ball, turn it towards your left side. (See note below)

4. Count how many times in a row you hit the ball to the left before it bounces more than once. This is your score.

5. When the ball doesn't turn to the left or bounces more than once: stop the drill; write down your score in **"Today's Scores"**; and start the drill again at step 1.

6. Do this drill for 5 minutes.

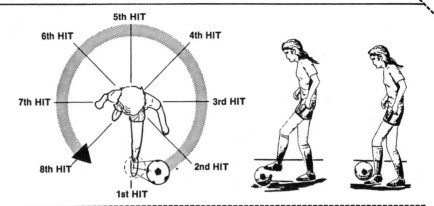

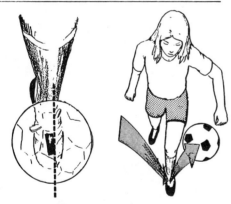

NOTE: To turn the ball to the left, hit the ball a little to the right of its midline.

Today's Scores

YOUR GOAL: A score of 8 or more hits in a row

HITS																					

How To Watch Your Score Improve

1. Write down your score for today. The first day you do this drill, write your score by **DAY 1**, Write you score for the second day by **DAY 2**, and so on.

2. Did you meet your goal?

NO!

Erase **"Today's Scores"** and do this drill again the next time you **PRACTICE SOCCER BY YOURSELF.**

YES!

WELL DONE! The next time you **PRACTICE SOCCER BY YOURSELF** you can move up to the drill on the next page.

Also cut off the number on the top of this page. Then turn to the **PROGRESS CHART** at the end of the book.

DAY	SCORE	DAY	SCORE	DAY	SCORE
1		11		21	
2		12		22	
3		13		23	
4		14		24	
5		15		25	
6		16		26	
7		17		27	
8		18		28	
9		19		29	
10		20		30	

NOTES:

NO-BOUNCE JUGGLES TO THE RIGHT

What You Need To Do This Drill
- A small area of flat ground
- A soccer ball
- This page, a pencil and an eraser

How To Set Up For This Drill
A. No set up is needed.

How To Do This Drill

1. Stand with the ball at your feet.

2. Lift the ball off the ground with your foot.

3. No-bounce juggle using your right foot or leg only. Each time you hit the ball, turn it towards your right side.

4. Count how many times in a row you hit the ball to your right before it falls to the ground. This is your score.

5. When the ball doesn't turn to the left or touches the ground: stop the drill; write down your score in **"Today's Scores"**; and start the drill again at step 1.

6. Do this drill for 5 minutes.

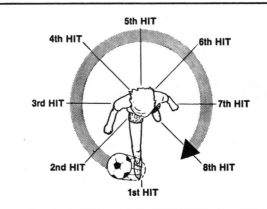

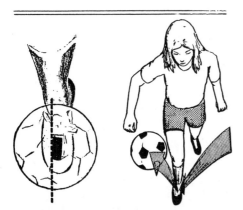

NOTE: To turn the ball to the right, hit the ball a little to the left of its midline.

Today's Scores

YOUR GOAL: A score of 4 or more hits in a row

HITS																			

How To Watch Your Score Improve

1. Write down your score for today. The first day you do this drill, write your score by **DAY 1**, Write you score for the second day by **DAY 2**, and so on.

2. Did you meet your goal?

NO!

Erase **"Today's Scores"** and do this drill again the next time you **PRACTICE SOCCER BY YOURSELF.**

YES!

WELL DONE! The next time you **PRACTICE SOCCER BY YOURSELF** you can move up to the drill on the next page.

Also cut off the number on the top of this page. Then turn to the **PROGRESS CHART** at the end of the book.

DAY	SCORE
1	
2	
3	
4	
5	
6	
7	
8	
9	
10	

DAY	SCORE
11	
12	
13	
14	
15	
16	
17	
18	
19	
20	

DAY	SCORE
21	
22	
23	
24	
25	
26	
27	
28	
29	
30	

NOTES:

NO-BOUNCE JUGGLES TO THE LEFT

What You Need To Do This Drill
- A small area of flat ground
- A soccer ball
- This page, a pencil and an eraser

How To Set Up For This Drill
A. No set up is needed.

How To Do This Drill
1. Stand with the ball at your feet.

2. Lift the ball off the ground with your foot.

3. No-bounce juggle using your left foot or leg only. Each time you hit the ball, hit it towards your left side.

4. Count how many times in a row you hit the ball to your left before the ball falls to the ground. This is your score.

5. When the ball doesn't turn to the right or touches the ground: stop the drill; write down your score in **"Today's Scores"**; and start the drill again at step 1.

6. Do this drill for 5 minutes.

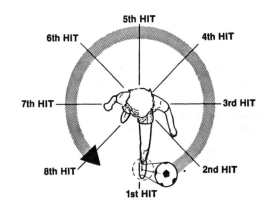

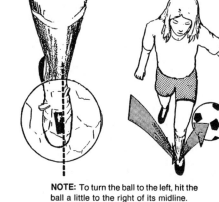

NOTE: To turn the ball to the left, hit the ball a little to the right of its midline.

Today's Scores

YOUR GOAL: A score of 4 or more hits in a row

HITS																						

How To Watch Your Score Improve

1. Write down your score for today. The first day you do this drill, write your score by **DAY 1**, Write you score for the second day by **DAY 2**, and so on.

2. Did you meet your goal?

NO!

Erase **"Today's Scores"** and do this drill again the next time you **PRACTICE SOCCER BY YOURSELF.**

YES!

WELL DONE! The next time you **PRACTICE SOCCER BY YOURSELF** you can move up to the drill on the next page.

Also cut off the number on the top of this page. Then turn to the **PROGRESS CHART** at the end of the book.

DAY	SCORE
1	
2	
3	
4	
5	
6	
7	
8	
9	
10	

DAY	SCORE
11	
12	
13	
14	
15	
16	
17	
18	
19	
20	

DAY	SCORE
21	
22	
23	
24	
25	
26	
27	
28	
29	
30	

NOTES:

HEAD JUGGLING — LIFT START

What You Need To Do This Drill
- A small area of flat ground
- A soccer ball
- This page, a pencil and an eraser

How To Set Up For This Drill
A. No set up is needed.

How To Do This Drill

1. Stand with the ball at your feet.

2. Lift the ball off the ground with your foot and kick the ball straight up, higher than your head.

3. As the ball falls, head it into the air.

4. Head it as many times as you can before it falls to the ground.

5. Count how many times you head the ball. This is your score.

When the ball touches the ground: stop the drill; write down your score in **"Today's Scores"**; start again at **step 1.**

6. Do this drill for 5 minutes.

NOTE: When you hit the ball with your head;

a. be sure to hit the ball with the top of your forehead. Hitting the ball with your head won't hurt you if you use your forehead.

b. keep your eyes open and watch the ball as your head hits it.

c. keep your mouth shut.

d. swing your body from the waist to get good power.

Today's Scores

YOUR GOAL: A score of 6 or more hits

	1	2	3	4	5	6	7	8	9	10	11	12	13	14	15	16	17	18	19	20
NUMBER OF HITS																				

How To Watch Your Score Improve

1. Write down your score for today. The first day you do this drill, write your score by **DAY 1**, Write you score for the second day by **DAY 2**, and so on.

2. Did you meet your goal?

NO!

Erase **"Today's Scores"** and do this drill again the next time you **PRACTICE SOCCER BY YOURSELF.**

YES!

WELL DONE! The next time you **PRACTICE SOCCER BY YOURSELF** you can move up to the drill on the next page.

Also cut off the number on the top of this page. Then turn to the **PROGRESS CHART** at the end of the book.

DAY	SCORE
1	
2	
3	
4	
5	
6	
7	
8	
9	
10	

DAY	SCORE
11	
12	
13	
14	
15	
16	
17	
18	
19	
20	

DAY	SCORE
21	
22	
23	
24	
25	
26	
27	
28	
29	
30	

NOTES:

ROTATION JUGGLING — RIGHT FOOT, RIGHT THIGH

What You Need To Do This Drill

- A small area of flat ground
- A soccer ball
- This page, a pencil and an eraser

How To Set Up For This Drill

A. No set up is needed.

How To Do This Drill

1. Stand with the ball at your feet.

2. Lift the ball with your foot.

3. No-bounce juggle, touching the ball in the following order:
Lift start--- Right foot--- Right thigh--- Right foot--- Right thigh--- as many times as you can.

4. Count how many times in a row you juggle the ball in the correct order before it touches the ground.

5. When the ball touches the ground: stop the drill; write down your score in **"Today's Scores"**; and start the drill again at step 1.

6. Do this drill for 5 minutes.

------- LIFT START ------- Right Foot

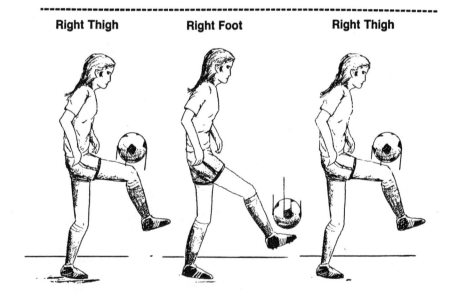

Right Thigh   Right Foot   Right Thigh

Today's Scores

YOUR GOAL: A score of 8 or more hits in a row

HITS																

How To Watch Your Score Improve

1. Write down your score for today. The first day you do this drill, write your score by **DAY 1**, Write you score for the second day by **DAY 2**, and so on.

2. Did you meet your goal?

NO!

Erase **"Today's Scores"** and do this drill again the next time you **PRACTICE SOCCER BY YOURSELF.**

YES!

WELL DONE! The next time you **PRACTICE SOCCER BY YOURSELF** you can move up to the drill on the next page.

Also cut off the number on the top of this page. Then turn to the **PROGRESS CHART** at the end of the book.

DAY	SCORE		DAY	SCORE		DAY	SCORE
1			11			21	
2			12			22	
3			13			23	
4			14			24	
5			15			25	
6			16			26	
7			17			27	
8			18			28	
9			19			29	
10			20			30	

NOTES:

ROTATION JUGGLING — LEFT FOOT, LEFT THIGH

What You Need To Do This Drill

- A small area of flat ground
- A soccer ball
- This page, a pencil and an eraser

How To Set Up For This Drill

A. No set up is needed.

How To Do This Drill

1. Stand with the ball at your feet.

2. Lift the ball with your foot.

3. No-bounce juggle, touching the ball in the following order:
Lift start--- Left foot--- Left thigh--- Left foot--- Left thigh--- as many times as you can.

4. Count how many times in a row you juggle the ball in the correct order before it touches the ground.

5. When the ball touches the ground: stop the drill; write down your score in **"Today's Scores"**; and start the drill again at step 1.

6. Do this drill for 5 minutes.

------- LIFT START -------

| Left Foot | Left Thigh | Left Foot |

Today's Scores

YOUR GOAL: A score of 8 or more hits in a row

HITS																		

How To Watch Your Score Improve

1. Write down your score for today. The first day you do this drill, write your score by **DAY 1**, Write you score for the second day by **DAY 2**, and so on.

2. Did you meet your goal?

NO!

Erase **"Today's Scores"** and do this drill again the next time you **PRACTICE SOCCER BY YOURSELF.**

YES!

WELL DONE! The next time you **PRACTICE SOCCER BY YOURSELF** you can move up to the drill on the next page.

Also cut off the number on the top of this page. Then turn to the **PROGRESS CHART** at the end of the book.

DAY	SCORE
1	
2	
3	
4	
5	
6	
7	
8	
9	
10	

DAY	SCORE
11	
12	
13	
14	
15	
16	
17	
18	
19	
20	

DAY	SCORE
21	
22	
23	
24	
25	
26	
27	
28	
29	
30	

NOTES:

ROTATION JUGGLING — RIGHT FOOT, RIGHT THIGH, HEAD

What You Need To Do This Drill

- A small area of flat ground
- A soccer ball
- This page, a pencil and an eraser

How To Set Up For This Drill

A. No set up is needed.

How To Do This Drill

1. Stand with the ball at your feet.

2. Lift the ball with your foot.

3. No-bounce juggle, touching the ball in the following order:
Lift start--- Right foot--- Right thigh--- Head--- Right foot--- Right thigh--- as many times as you can.

4. Count how many times in a row you juggle the ball in the correct order before it touches the ground.

5. When the ball touches the ground: stop the drill; write down your score in **"Today's Scores"**; and start the drill again at step 1.

6. Do this drill for 5 minutes.

------- LIFT START -------

Right Foot   **Right Thigh**

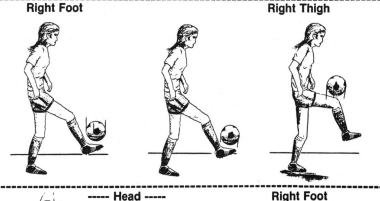

----- Head -----   **Right Foot**

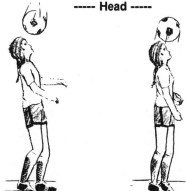

Today's Scores

YOUR GOAL: A score of 6 or more hits in a row

HITS																					

How To Watch Your Score Improve

1. Write down your score for today. The first day you do this drill, write your score by **DAY 1**, Write you score for the second day by **DAY 2**, and so on.

2. Did you meet your goal?

NO!

Erase **"Today's Scores"** and do this drill again the next time you **PRACTICE SOCCER BY YOURSELF.**

YES!

WELL DONE! The next time you **PRACTICE SOCCER BY YOURSELF** you can move up to the drill on the next page.

Also cut off the number on the top of this page. Then turn to the **PROGRESS CHART** at the end of the book.

DAY	SCORE	DAY	SCORE	DAY	SCORE
1		11		21	
2		12		22	
3		13		23	
4		14		24	
5		15		25	
6		16		26	
7		17		27	
8		18		28	
9		19		29	
10		20		30	

NOTES:

ROTATION JUGGLING — LEFT FOOT, LEFT THIGH, HEAD

What You Need To Do This Drill
- A small area of flat ground
- A soccer ball
- This page, a pencil and an eraser

How To Set Up For This Drill
A. No set up is needed.

How To Do This Drill

1. Stand with the ball at your feet.

2. Lift the ball with your foot.

3. No-bounce juggle, touching the ball in the following order:

Lift start--- Left foot--- Left thigh--- Head--- Left foot--- Left thigh--- as many times as you can.

4. Count how many times in a row you juggle the ball in the correct order before it touches the ground.

5. When the ball touches the ground: stop the drill; write down your score in **"Today's Scores"**; and start the drill again at step 1.

6. Do this drill for 5 minutes.

---------- Lift Start ----------

Left Foot   Left Thigh

····· Head ·····   Left Foot

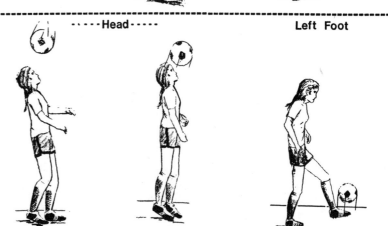

Today's Scores

YOUR GOAL: A score of 6 or more hits in a row

HITS																					

How To Watch Your Score Improve

1. Write down your score for today. The first day you do this drill, write your score by **DAY 1**, Write you score for the second day by **DAY 2**, and so on.

2. Did you meet your goal?

NO!

Erase **"Today's Scores"** and do this drill again the next time you **PRACTICE SOCCER BY YOURSELF.**

YES!

WELL DONE! The next time you **PRACTICE SOCCER BY YOURSELF** you can move up to the drill on the next page.

Also cut off the number on the top of this page. Then turn to the **PROGRESS CHART** at the end of the book.

DAY	SCORE	DAY	SCORE	DAY	SCORE
1		11		21	
2		12		22	
3		13		23	
4		14		24	
5		15		25	
6		16		26	
7		17		27	
8		18		28	
9		19		29	
10		20		30	

NOTES:

ROTATION JUGGLING — RIGHT & LEFT SIDES

What You Need To Do This Drill
- A small area of flat ground
- A soccer ball
- This page, a pencil and an eraser

How To Set Up For This Drill
A. No set up is needed.

How To Do This Drill

1. Stand with the ball at your feet.

2. Lift the ball with your foot.

3. No-bounce juggle, touching the ball in the following order:

Lift start--- Right foot--- Right thigh--- Head--- Left foot--- Left thigh--- Head--- Right Foot--- Right Thigh--- as many times as you can.

4. Count how many times in a row you juggle the ball in the correct order before it touches the ground.

5. When the ball touches the ground: stop the drill; write down your score in **"Today's Scores"**; and start the drill again at step 1.

6. Do this drill for 5 minutes.

------- LIFT START -------

Right Foot   Right Thigh

----- Head -----   Left Foot   Left Thigh   ----- Head -----   Right Foot

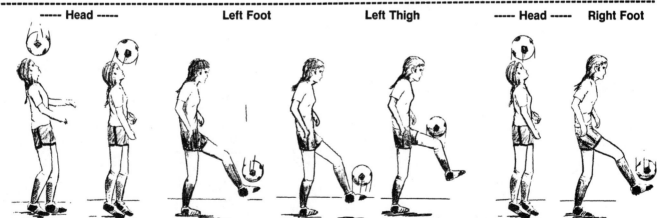

Today's Scores

YOUR GOAL: A score of 8 or more hits in a row

HITS																			

How To Watch Your Score Improve

1. Write down your score for today. The first day you do this drill, write your score by **DAY 1**, Write you score for the second day by **DAY 2**, and so on.

2. Did you meet your goal?

NO!

Erase **"Today's Scores"** and do this drill again the next time you **PRACTICE SOCCER BY YOURSELF.**

YES!

WELL DONE! The next time you **PRACTICE SOCCER BY YOURSELF** you can move up to the drill on the next page.

Also cut off the number on the top of this page. Then turn to the **PROGRESS CHART** at the end of the book.

DAY	SCORE
1	
2	
3	
4	
5	
6	
7	
8	
9	
10	

DAY	SCORE
11	
12	
13	
14	
15	
16	
17	
18	
19	
20	

DAY	SCORE
21	
22	
23	
24	
25	
26	
27	
28	
29	
30	

NOTES:

HEAD JUGGLING — LIFT START

What You Need To Do This Drill
- A small area of flat ground
- A soccer ball
- This page, a pencil and an eraser

How To Set Up For This Drill
A. No set up is needed.

How To Do This Drill

1. Stand with the ball at your feet.

2. Lift the ball off the ground with your foot and kick the ball straight up, higher than your head.

3. As the ball falls, head it into the air.

4. Head it as many times as you can before it falls to the ground.

5. Count how many times you head the ball. This is your score.

When the ball touches the ground: stop the drill; write down your score in **"Today's Scores"**; start again at **step 1.**

6. Do this drill for 5 minutes.

NOTE: When you hit the ball with your head;

a. be sure to hit the ball with the top of your forehead. Hitting the ball with your head won't hurt you if you use your forehead.

b. keep your eyes open and watch the ball as your head hits it.

c. keep your mouth shut.

d. swing your body from the waist to get good power.

Today's Scores

YOUR GOAL: A score of 7 or more hits

	1	2	3	4	5	6	7	8	9	10	11	12	13	14	15	16	17	18	19	20
NUMBER OF HITS																				

How To Watch Your Score Improve

1. Write down your score for today. The first day you do this drill, write your score by **DAY 1**, Write you score for the second day by **DAY 2**, and so on.

2. Did you meet your goal?

NO!

Erase **"Today's Scores"** and do this drill again the next time you **PRACTICE SOCCER BY YOURSELF.**

YES!

WELL DONE! The next time you **PRACTICE SOCCER BY YOURSELF** you can move up to the drill on the next page.

Also cut off the number on the top of this page. Then turn to the **PROGRESS CHART** at the end of the book.

DAY	SCORE
1	
2	
3	
4	
5	
6	
7	
8	
9	
10	

DAY	SCORE
11	
12	
13	
14	
15	
16	
17	
18	
19	
20	

DAY	SCORE
21	
22	
23	
24	
25	
26	
27	
28	
29	
30	

NOTES:

...DRIBBLING THE BALL?

Picture yourself in a soccer game. The ball has just been passed to you and a member of the other team is close to you.

He is moving in too quickly for you to find an open teammate and then pass the ball.

Now, think about what you might do...
...You could pass the ball where one of your teammates should be—sometimes this works. You could dribble the ball and then find someone to receive a pass—this is probably the better idea.

You've been practicing your dribbling skills so you have a good chance of getting by the other player. Go for it!

In the following drills, you will learn how to dribble the ball with the inside and outside of either foot, and you will learn several ways to turn around with the ball under control.

DRIBBLING (PULLBACK TURNS)

What You Need To Do This Drill

- A small area of flat ground
- A soccer ball
- 9 markers (boxes, cones, cups)
- This page, a pencil and an eraser

How To Set Up For This Drill

A. Set five markers in a row as shown in the diagram.

B. Set two markers at each end of the row as shown in the diagram.

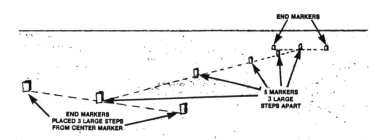

END MARKERS

5 MARKERS
3 LARGE
STEPS APART

END MARKERS
PLACED 3 LARGE STEPS
FROM CENTER MARKER

How To Do This Drill

1. Place the ball at your feet near marker 1.

2. Using your feet move (dribble) the ball around marker 1, 2, 3, 4, and 5. If you hit a marker or the ball goes over the boundary line, start the drill again at marker 1.

3. When you get past marker 5, step on the ball, pull it behind you and turn around.

4. Using your feet move (dribble) the ball around marker 5, 4, 3, 2, and 1. If you hit a marker or the ball goes over the boundary line, start the drill again at marker 1.

5. If you dribbled the ball from marker 1 through 5 and back without hitting a marker or going out of bounds, give yourself **1 point** in **"Today's Scores."**

6. Do this for 5 minutes.

7. When you have finished count up your points for the day. This is your score.

NOTE: When you dribble, keep the ball close to your feet for good control

NOTE: When you dribble, bend slightly (at the waist) over the ball

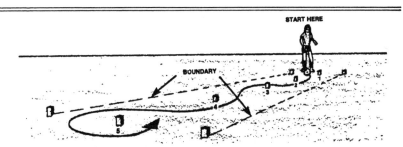

START HERE

BOUNDARY

| START | RIGHT TURN | LEFT TURN | RIGHT TURN |

STEP ON BALL   PULL IT BEHIND   TURN AROUND

Today's Scores

YOUR GOAL: A score of 5 or more points

POINTS	1	2	3	4	5	6	7	8	9	10	11	12	13	14	15	16	17	18	19	20	TOTAL

How To Watch Your Score Improve

1. Write down your score for today. The first day you do this drill, write your score by **DAY 1**, Write you score for the second day by **DAY 2**, and so on.

2. Did you meet your goal?

NO!

Erase **"Today's Scores"** and do this drill again the next time you **PRACTICE SOCCER BY YOURSELF.**

YES!

WELL DONE! The next time you **PRACTICE SOCCER BY YOURSELF** you can move up to the drill on the next page.

Also cut off the number on the top of this page. Then turn to the **PROGRESS CHART** at the end of the book.

DAY	SCORE
1	
2	
3	
4	
5	
6	
7	
8	
9	
10	

DAY	SCORE
11	
12	
13	
14	
15	
16	
17	
18	
19	
20	

DAY	SCORE
21	
22	
23	
24	
25	
26	
27	
28	
29	
30	

NOTES:

DRIBBLING (HEEL TURNS)

What You Need To Do This Drill

- A small area of flat ground
- A soccer ball
- 9 markers (boxes, cones, cups)
- This page, a pencil and an eraser

How To Set Up For This Drill

A. Set five markers in a row as shown in the diagram.

B. Set two markers at each end of the row as shown in the diagram.

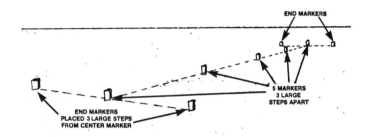

END MARKERS

5 MARKERS
3 LARGE
STEPS APART

END MARKERS
PLACED 3 LARGE STEPS
FROM CENTER MARKER

How To Do This Drill

1. Place the ball at your feet near marker 1.

2. Using your feet move (dribble) the ball around marker 1, 2, 3, 4, and 5. If you hit a marker or the ball goes over the boundary line, start the drill again at marker 1.

3. When you get past marker 5, step over the ball, stop it with your heel and turn around.

4. Using your feet move (dribble) the ball around marker 5, 4, 3, 2, and 1. If you hit a marker or the ball goes over the boundary line, start the drill again at marker 1.

5. If you dribbled the ball from marker 1 through 5 and back without hitting a marker or going out of bounds, give yourself **1 point** in **"Today's Scores."**

6. Do this for 5 minutes.

7. When you have finished count up your points for the day. This is your score.

NOTE: When you dribble, keep the ball close to your feet for good control

NOTE: When you dribble, bend slightly (at the waist) over the ball

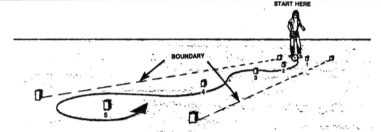

START HERE

BOUNDARY

START | RIGHT TURN | LEFT TURN | RIGHT TURN

STOP THE BALL
WITH YOUR HEEL

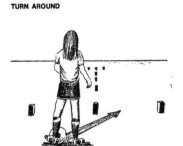

TURN AROUND

Today's Scores

YOUR GOAL: A score of 5 or more points

	1	2	3	4	5	6	7	8	9	10	11	12	13	14	15	16	17	18	19	20	TOTAL
POINTS																					

How To Watch Your Score Improve

1. Write down your score for today. The first day you do this drill, write your score by **DAY 1**, Write you score for the second day by **DAY 2**, and so on.

2. Did you meet your goal?

NO!

Erase **"Today's Scores"** and do this drill again the next time you **PRACTICE SOCCER BY YOURSELF.**

YES!

WELL DONE! The next time you **PRACTICE SOCCER BY YOURSELF** you can move up to the drill on the next page.

Also cut off the number on the top of this page. Then turn to the **PROGRESS CHART** at the end of the book.

DAY	SCORE
1	
2	
3	
4	
5	
6	
7	
8	
9	
10	

DAY	SCORE
11	
12	
13	
14	
15	
16	
17	
18	
19	
20	

DAY	SCORE
21	
22	
23	
24	
25	
26	
27	
28	
29	
30	

NOTES:

DRIBBLING (SQUARE TURNS)

What You Need To Do This Drill

- A small area of flat ground
- A soccer ball
- 9 markers (boxes, cones, cups)
- This page, a pencil and an eraser

How To Set Up For This Drill

A. Set five markers in a row as shown in the diagram.

B. Set two markers at each end of the row as shown in the diagram.

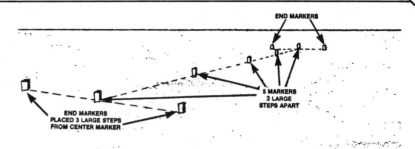

How To Do This Drill

1. Place the ball at your feet near marker 1.

2. Using your feet move (dribble) the ball around marker 1, 2, 3, 4, and 5. If you hit a marker or the ball goes over the boundary line, start the drill again at marker 1.

3. When you get past marker 5, step over the ball with your left foot, then push the ball behind your left foot with your right foot and turn around.

4. Using your feet move (dribble) the ball around marker 5, 4, 3, 2, and 1. If you hit a marker or the ball goes over the boundary line, start the drill again at marker 1.

5. If you dribbled the ball from marker 1 through 5 and back without hitting a marker or going out of bounds, give yourself **1 point** in **"Today's Scores."**

6. Do this for 5 minutes.

7. When you have finished count up your points for the day. This is your score.

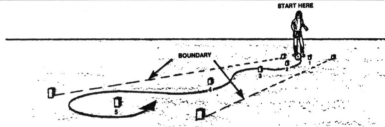

NOTE: When you dribble, keep the ball close to your feet for good control

NOTE: When you dribble, bend slightly (at the waist) over the ball

STEP OVER THE BALL

PUSH IT BEHIND YOUR FOOT

TURN AROUND

Today's Scores

YOUR GOAL: A score of 5 or more points

	1	2	3	4	5	6	7	8	9	10	11	12	13	14	15	16	17	18	19	20	TOTAL
POINTS																					

How To Watch Your Score Improve

1. Write down your score for today. The first day you do this drill, write your score by **DAY 1**, Write you score for the second day by **DAY 2**, and so on.

2. Did you meet your goal?

NO!

Erase **"Today's Scores"** and do this drill again the next time you **PRACTICE SOCCER BY YOURSELF.**

YES!

WELL DONE! The next time you **PRACTICE SOCCER BY YOURSELF** you can move up to the drill on the next page.

Also cut off the number on the top of this page. Then turn to the **PROGRESS CHART** at the end of the book.

DAY	SCORE	DAY	SCORE	DAY	SCORE
1		11		21	
2		12		22	
3		13		23	
4		14		24	
5		15		25	
6		16		26	
7		17		27	
8		18		28	
9		19		29	
10		20		30	

NOTES:

RIGHT FOOT DRIBBLING (PULLBACK TURNS)

What You Need To Do This Drill

- A small area of flat ground
- A soccer ball
- 9 markers (boxes, cones, cups)
- This page, a pencil and an eraser

How To Set Up For This Drill

A. Set five markers in a row as shown in the diagram.

B. Set two markers at each end of the row as shown in the diagram.

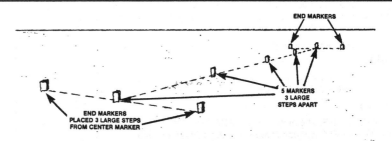

How To Do This Drill

1. Place the ball at your feet near marker 1.

2. Using your right foot only dribble the ball around marker 1, 2, 3, 4, and 5. If you hit a marker or the ball goes over the boundary line, start the drill again at marker 1.

3. When you get past marker 5, step on the ball, pull it behind you and turn around.

4. Using your right foot only dribble the ball around marker 5, 4, 3, 2, and 1. If you hit a marker or the ball goes over the boundary line, start the drill again at marker 1.

5. If you dribbled the ball from marker 1 through 5 and back without hitting a marker or going out of bounds, give yourself **1 point** in **"Today's Scores."**

6. Do this for 5 minutes.

7. When you have finished count up your points for the day. This is your score.

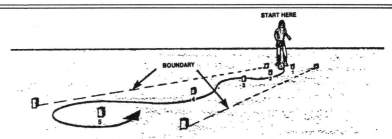

Today's Scores

YOUR GOAL: A score of 5 or more points

	1	2	3	4	5	6	7	8	9	10	11	12	13	14	15	16	17	18	19	20	TOTAL
POINTS																					

How To Watch Your Score Improve

1. Write down your score for today. The first day you do this drill, write your score by **DAY 1**, Write you score for the second day by **DAY 2**, and so on.

2. Did you meet your goal?

NO!

Erase **"Today's Scores"** and do this drill again the next time you **PRACTICE SOCCER BY YOURSELF.**

YES!

WELL DONE! The next time you **PRACTICE SOCCER BY YOURSELF** you can move up to the drill on the next page.

Also cut off the number on the top of this page. Then turn to the **PROGRESS CHART** at the end of the book.

DAY	SCORE	DAY	SCORE	DAY	SCORE
1		11		21	
2		12		22	
3		13		23	
4		14		24	
5		15		25	
6		16		26	
7		17		27	
8		18		28	
9		19		29	
10		20		30	

NOTES:

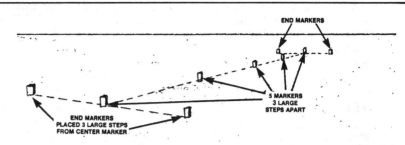

LEFT FOOT DRIBBLING (PULLBACK TURNS)

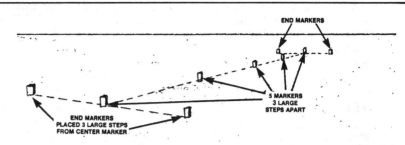

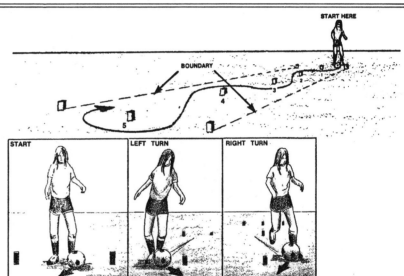

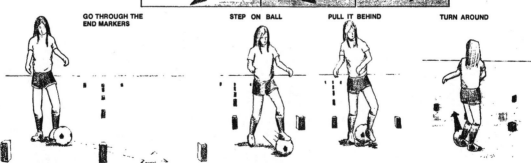

LEFT FOOT DRIBBLING (PULLBACK TURNS)

What You Need To Do This Drill

- A small area of flat ground
- A soccer ball
- 9 markers (boxes, cones, cups)
- This page, a pencil and an eraser

How To Set Up For This Drill

A. Set five markers in a row as shown in the diagram.

B. Set two markers at each end of the row as shown in the diagram.

END MARKERS

5 MARKERS
3 LARGE
STEPS APART

END MARKERS
PLACED 3 LARGE STEPS
FROM CENTER MARKER

How To Do This Drill

1. Place the ball at your feet near marker 1.

2. Using your left foot only dribble the ball around marker 1, 2, 3, 4, and 5. If you hit a marker or the ball goes over the boundary line, start the drill again at marker 1.

3. When you get past marker 5, step on the ball, pull it behind you and turn around.

4. Using your left foot only dribble the ball around marker 5, 4, 3, 2, and 1. If you hit a marker or the ball goes over the boundary line, start the drill again at marker 1.

5. If you dribbled the ball from marker 1 through 5 and back without hitting a marker or going out of bounds, give yourself **1 point** in **"Today's Scores."**

6. Do this for 5 minutes.

7. When you have finished count up your points for the day. This is your score.

START HERE

BOUNDARY

START   LEFT TURN   RIGHT TURN

GO THROUGH THE END MARKERS

STEP ON BALL   PULL IT BEHIND   TURN AROUND

Today's Scores

YOUR GOAL: A score of 5 or more points

	1	2	3	4	5	6	7	8	9	10	11	12	13	14	15	16	17	18	19	20	TOTAL
POINTS																					

145

How To Watch Your Score Improve

1. Write down your score for today. The first day you do this drill, write your score by **DAY 1**, Write you score for the second day by **DAY 2**, and so on.

2. Did you meet your goal?

NO!

Erase **"Today's Scores"** and do this drill again the next time you **PRACTICE SOCCER BY YOURSELF.**

YES!

WELL DONE! The next time you **PRACTICE SOCCER BY YOURSELF** you can move up to the drill on the next page.

Also cut off the number on the top of this page. Then turn to the **PROGRESS CHART** at the end of the book.

DAY	SCORE		DAY	SCORE		DAY	SCORE
1			11			21	
2			12			22	
3			13			23	
4			14			24	
5			15			25	
6			16			26	
7			17			27	
8			18			28	
9			19			29	
10			20			30	

NOTES:

RIGHT FOOT DRIBBLING (HEEL TURNS)

What You Need To Do This Drill

- A small area of flat ground
- A soccer ball
- 9 markers (boxes, cones, cups)
- This page, a pencil and an eraser

How To Set Up For This Drill

A. Set five markers in a row as shown in the diagram.

B. Set two markers at each end of the row as shown in the diagram.

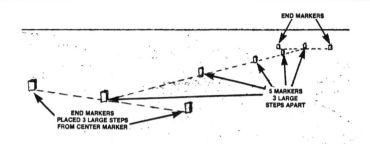

How To Do This Drill

1. Place the ball at your feet near marker 1.

2. Using your right foot only dribble the ball around marker 1, 2, 3, 4, and 5. If you hit a marker or the ball goes over the boundary line, start the drill again at marker 1.

3. When you get past marker 5, step over the ball, stop it with your heel and turn around.

4. Using your right foot only dribble the ball around marker 5, 4, 3, 2, and 1. If you hit a marker or the ball goes over the boundary line, start the drill again at marker 1.

5. If you dribbled the ball from marker 1 through 5 and back without hitting a marker or going out of bounds, give your self **1 point** in **"Today's Scores."**

6. Do this for 5 minutes.

7. When you have finished count up your points for the day. This is your score.

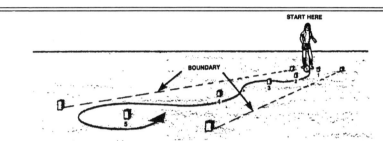

Today's Scores

YOUR GOAL: A score of 5 or more points

	1	2	3	4	5	6	7	8	9	10	11	12	13	14	15	16	17	18	19	20	TOTAL
POINTS																					

How To Watch Your Score Improve

1. Write down your score for today. The first day you do this drill, write your score by **DAY 1**, Write you score for the second day by **DAY 2**, and so on.

2. Did you meet your goal?

NO!

Erase **"Today's Scores"** and do this drill again the next time you **PRACTICE SOCCER BY YOURSELF.**

YES!

WELL DONE! The next time you **PRACTICE SOCCER BY YOURSELF** you can move up to the drill on the next page.

Also cut off the number on the top of this page. Then turn to the **PROGRESS CHART** at the end of the book.

DAY	SCORE		DAY	SCORE		DAY	SCORE
1			11			21	
2			12			22	
3			13			23	
4			14			24	
5			15			25	
6			16			26	
7			17			27	
8			18			28	
9			19			29	
10			20			30	

NOTES:

LEFT FOOT DRIBBLING (HEEL TURNS)

What You Need To Do This Drill

- A small area of flat ground
- A soccer ball
- 9 markers (boxes, cones, cups)
- This page, a pencil and an eraser

How To Set Up For This Drill

A. Set five markers in a row as shown in the diagram.

B. Set two markers at each end of the row as shown in the diagram.

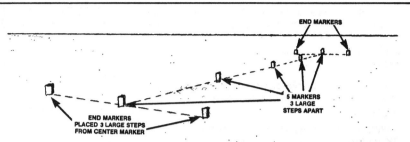

How To Do This Drill

1. Place the ball at your feet near marker 1.

2. Using your left foot only dribble the ball around marker 1, 2, 3, 4, and 5. If you hit a marker or the ball goes over the boundary line, start the drill again at marker 1.

3. When you get past marker 5, step over the ball, stop it with your heel and turn around.

4. Using your left foot only dribble the ball around marker 1, 2, 3, 4, and 5. If you hit a marker or the ball goes over the boundary line, start the drill again at marker 1.

5. If you dribbled the ball from marker 1 through 5 and back without hitting a marker or going out of bounds, give yourself **1 point** in **"Today's Scores."**

6. Do this for 5 minutes.

7. When you have finished count up your points for the day. This is your score.

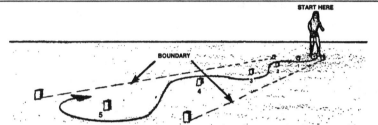

Today's Scores

YOUR GOAL: A score of 5 or more points

	1	2	3	4	5	6	7	8	9	10	11	12	13	14	15	16	17	18	19	20	TOTAL
POINTS																					

How To Watch Your Score Improve

1. Write down your score for today. The first day you do this drill, write your score by **DAY 1**, Write you score for the second day by **DAY 2**, and so on.

2. Did you meet your goal?

NO!

Erase **"Today's Scores"** and do this drill again the next time you **PRACTICE SOCCER BY YOURSELF**.

YES!

WELL DONE! The next time you **PRACTICE SOCCER BY YOURSELF** you can move up to the drill on the next page.

Also cut off the number on the top of this page. Then turn to the **PROGRESS CHART** at the end of the book.

DAY	SCORE		DAY	SCORE		DAY	SCORE
1			11			21	
2			12			22	
3			13			23	
4			14			24	
5			15			25	
6			16			26	
7			17			27	
8			18			28	
9			19			29	
10			20			30	

NOTES:

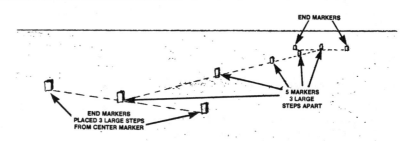

RIGHT FOOT DRIBBLING (SQUARE TURNS)

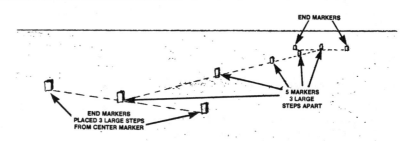

What You Need To Do This Drill

- A small area of flat ground
- A soccer ball
- 9 markers (boxes, cones, cups)
- This page, a pencil and an eraser

How To Set Up For This Drill

A. Set five markers in a row as shown in the diagram.

B. Set two markers at each end of the row as shown in the diagram.

END MARKERS

5 MARKERS
3 LARGE
STEPS APART

END MARKERS
PLACED 3 LARGE STEPS
FROM CENTER MARKER

How To Do This Drill

1. Place the ball at your feet near marker 1.

2. Using your right foot only dribble the ball around marker 1, 2, 3, 4, and 5. If you hit a marker or the ball goes over the boundary line, start the drill again at marker 1.

3. When you get past marker 5, step over the ball with your left foot, then push the ball behind your left foot with your right foot and turn around.

4. Using your right foot only dribble the ball around marker 5, 4, 3, 2, and 1. If you hit a marker or the ball goes over the boundary line, start the drill again at marker 1.

5. If you dribbled the ball from marker 1 through 5 and back without hitting a marker or going out of bounds, give yourself **1 point** in **"Today's Scores."**

6. Do this for 5 minutes.

7. When you have finished count up your points for the day. This is your score.

NOTE: When you dribble, keep the ball close to your feet for good control

NOTE: When you dribble, bend slightly (at the waist) over the ball

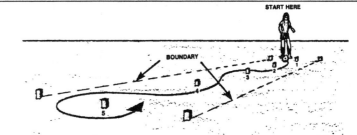

START HERE

BOUNDARY

START | RIGHT TURN | LEFT TURN | RIGHT TURN

STEP OVER THE BALL | PUSH IT BEHIND YOUR FOOT | TURN AROUND

Today's Scores

YOUR GOAL: A score of 5 or more points

	1	2	3	4	5	6	7	8	9	10	11	12	13	14	15	16	17	18	19	20	TOTAL
POINTS																					

How To Watch Your Score Improve

1. Write down your score for today. The first day you do this drill, write your score by **DAY 1**, Write you score for the second day by **DAY 2**, and so on.

2. Did you meet your goal?

NO!

Erase **"Today's Scores"** and do this drill again the next time you **PRACTICE SOCCER BY YOURSELF.**

YES!

WELL DONE! The next time you **PRACTICE SOCCER BY YOURSELF** you can move up to the drill on the next page.

Also cut off the number on the top of this page. Then turn to the **PROGRESS CHART** at the end of the book.

DAY	SCORE
1	
2	
3	
4	
5	
6	
7	
8	
9	
10	

DAY	SCORE
11	
12	
13	
14	
15	
16	
17	
18	
19	
20	

DAY	SCORE
21	
22	
23	
24	
25	
26	
27	
28	
29	
30	

NOTES:

LEFT FOOT DRIBBLING (SQUARE TURNS)

What You Need To Do This Drill

- A small area of flat ground
- A soccer ball
- 9 markers (boxes, cones, cups)
- This page, a pencil and an eraser

How To Set Up For This Drill

A. Set five markers in a row as shown in the diagram.

B. Set two markers at each end of the row as shown in the diagram.

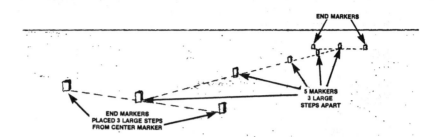

How To Do This Drill

1. Place the ball at your feet near marker 1.

2. Using your left foot only dribble the ball around marker 1, 2, 3, 4, and 5. If you hit a marker or the ball goes over the boundary line, start the drill again at marker 1.

3. When you get past marker 5, step over the ball with your right foot, then push the ball behind your right foot with your left foot and turn around.

4. Using your left foot dribble the ball around marker 5, 4, 3, 2, and 1. If you hit a marker or the ball goes over the boundary line, start the drill again at marker 1.

5. If you dribbled the ball from marker 1 through 5 and back without hitting a marker or going out of bounds, give yourself **1 point** in **"Today's Scores."**

6. Do this for 5 minutes.

7. When you have finished count up your points for the day. This is your score.

NOTE: When you dribble, keep the ball close to your feet for good control

NOTE: When you dribble, bend slightly (at the waist) over the ball

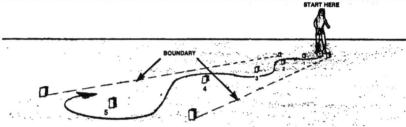

Today's Scores

YOUR GOAL: A score of 5 or more points

	1	2	3	4	5	6	7	8	9	10	11	12	13	14	15	16	17	18	19	20	TOTAL
POINTS																					

How To Watch Your Score Improve

1. Write down your score for today. The first day you do this drill, write your score by **DAY 1**, Write you score for the second day by **DAY 2**, and so on.

2. Did you meet your goal?

NO!

Erase **"Today's Scores"** and do this drill again the next time you **PRACTICE SOCCER BY YOURSELF.**

YES!

WELL DONE! The next time you **PRACTICE SOCCER BY YOURSELF** you can move up to the drill on the next page.

Also cut off the number on the top of this page. Then turn to the **PROGRESS CHART** at the end of the book.

DAY	SCORE
1	
2	
3	
4	
5	
6	
7	
8	
9	
10	

DAY	SCORE
11	
12	
13	
14	
15	
16	
17	
18	
19	
20	

DAY	SCORE
21	
22	
23	
24	
25	
26	
27	
28	
29	
30	

NOTES:

INSIDE OF THE FOOT DRIBBLING (HEEL TURNS)

What You Need To Do This Drill

- A small area of flat ground
- A soccer ball
- 9 markers (boxes, cones, cups)
- This page, a pencil and an eraser

How To Set Up For This Drill

A. Set five markers in a row as shown in the diagram.

B. Set two markers at each end of the row as shown in the diagram.

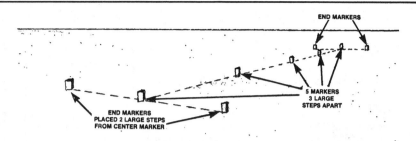

END MARKERS

5 MARKERS
3 LARGE
STEPS APART

END MARKERS
PLACED 2 LARGE STEPS
FROM CENTER MARKER

How To Do This Drill

1. Place the ball at your feet near marker 1.

2. Using the inside of both feet dribble the ball around marker 1, 2, 3, 4, and 5. If you hit a marker or the ball goes over the boundary line, start the drill again at marker 1.

3. When you get past marker 5, step over the ball, stop it with your heel and turn around.

4. Using the inside of both feet dribble the ball around marker 5, 4, 3, 2, and 1. If you hit a marker or the ball goes over the boundary line, start the drill again at marker 1.

5. If you dribbled the ball from marker 1 through 5 and back without hitting a marker or going out of bounds, give yourself **1 point** in **"Today's Scores."**

6. Do this for 5 minutes.

7. When you have finished count up your points for the day. This is your score.

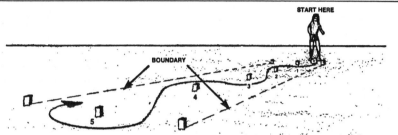

START HERE

BOUNDARY

NOTE: When you dribble, keep the ball close to your feet for good control

NOTE: When you dribble, bend slightly (at the waist) over the ball

START | LEFT TURN | RIGHT TURN | LEFT TURN

STOP THE BALL
WITH YOUR HEEL

TURN AROUND

Today's Scores

YOUR GOAL: A score of 8 or more points

	1	2	3	4	5	6	7	8	9	10	11	12	13	14	15	16	17	18	19	20	TOTAL
POINTS																					

How To Watch Your Score Improve

1. Write down your score for today. The first day you do this drill, write your score by **DAY 1,** Write you score for the second day by **DAY 2,** and so on.

2. Did you meet your goal?

NO!

Erase **"Today's Scores"** and do this drill again the next time you **PRACTICE SOCCER BY YOURSELF.**

YES!

WELL DONE! The next time you **PRACTICE SOCCER BY YOURSELF** you can move up to the drill on the next page.

Also cut off the number on the top of this page. Then turn to the **PROGRESS CHART** at the end of the book.

DAY	SCORE	DAY	SCORE	DAY	SCORE
1		11		21	
2		12		22	
3		13		23	
4		14		24	
5		15		25	
6		16		26	
7		17		27	
8		18		28	
9		19		29	
10		20		30	

NOTES:

OUTSIDE OF THE FOOT DRIBBLING (HEEL TURNS)

What You Need To Do This Drill

- A small area of flat ground
- A soccer ball
- 9 markers (boxes, cones, cups)
- This page, a pencil and an eraser

How To Set Up For This Drill

A. Set five markers in a row as shown in the diagram.

B. Set two markers at each end of the row as shown in the diagram.

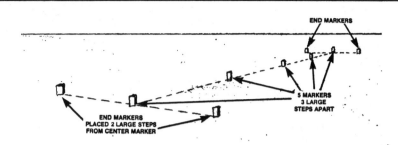

How To Do This Drill

1. Place the ball at your feet near marker 1.

2. Using the outside of both feet dribble the ball around marker 1, 2, 3, 4, and 5. If you hit a marker or the ball goes over the boundary line, start the drill again at marker 1.

3. When you get past marker 5, step over the ball, stop it with your heel and turn around.

4. Using the outside of both feet dribble the ball around marker 5, 4, 3, 2, and 1. If you hit a marker or the ball goes over the boundary line, start the drill again at marker 1.

5. If you dribbled the ball from marker 1 through 5 and back without hitting a marker or going out of bounds, give yourself **1 point** in **"Today's Scores."**

6. Do this for 5 minutes.

7. When you have finished count up your points for the day. This is your score.

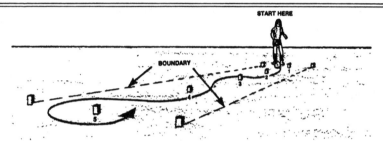

NOTE: When you dribble, keep the ball close to your feet for good control

NOTE: When you dribble, bend slightly (at the waist) over the ball

Today's Scores

YOUR GOAL: A score of 5 or more points

	1	2	3	4	5	6	7	8	9	10	11	12	13	14	15	16	17	18	19	20	TOTAL
POINTS																					

How To Watch Your Score Improve

1. Write down your score for today. The first day you do this drill, write your score by **DAY 1**, Write you score for the second day by **DAY 2**, and so on.

2. Did you meet your goal?

NO!

Erase **"Today's Scores"** and do this drill again the next time you **PRACTICE SOCCER BY YOURSELF.**

YES!

WELL DONE! The next time you **PRACTICE SOCCER BY YOURSELF** you can move up to the drill on the next page.

Also cut off the number on the top of this page. Then turn to the **PROGRESS CHART** at the end of the book.

DAY	SCORE	DAY	SCORE	DAY	SCORE
1		11		21	
2		12		22	
3		13		23	
4		14		24	
5		15		25	
6		16		26	
7		17		27	
8		18		28	
9		19		29	
10		20		30	

NOTES:

INSIDE OF THE FOOT DRIBBLING (PULLBACK TURNS)

What You Need To Do This Drill

- A small area of flat ground
- A soccer ball
- 9 markers (boxes, cones, cups)
- This page, a pencil and an eraser

How To Set Up For This Drill

A. Set five markers in a row as shown in the diagram.

B. Set two markers at each end of the row as shown in the diagram.

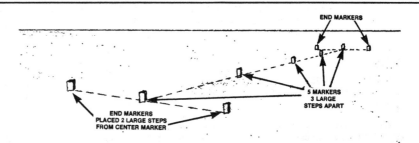

How To Do This Drill

1. Place the ball at your feet near marker 1.

2. Using the inside of both feet dribble the ball around marker 1, 2, 3, 4, and 5. If you hit a marker or the ball goes over the boundary line, start the drill again at marker 1.

3. When you get past marker 5, step on the ball, pull it behind you and turn around.

4. Using the inside of both feet dribble the ball around marker 5, 4, 3, 2, and 1. If you hit a marker or the ball goes over the boundary line, start the drill again at marker 1.

5. If you dribbled the ball from marker 1 through 5 and back without hitting a marker or going out of bounds, give yourself **1 point** in "**Today's Scores.**"

6. Do this for 5 minutes.

7. When you have finished count up your points for the day. This is your score.

NOTE: When you dribble, keep the ball close to your feet for good control

NOTE: When you dribble, bend slightly (at the waist) over the ball

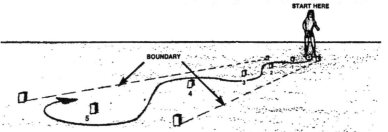

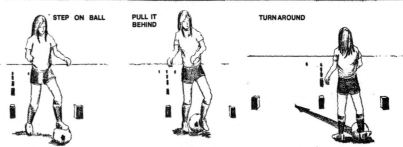

Today's Scores

YOUR GOAL: A score of 8 or more points

	1	2	3	4	5	6	7	8	9	10	11	12	13	14	15	16	17	18	19	20	TOTAL
POINTS																					

How To Watch Your Score Improve

1. Write down your score for today. The first day you do this drill, write your score by **DAY 1**, Write you score for the second day by **DAY 2**, and so on.

2. Did you meet your goal?

NO!

Erase **"Today's Scores"** and do this drill again the next time you **PRACTICE SOCCER BY YOURSELF.**

YES!

WELL DONE! The next time you **PRACTICE SOCCER BY YOURSELF** you can move up to the drill on the next page.

Also cut off the number on the top of this page. Then turn to the **PROGRESS CHART** at the end of the book.

DAY	SCORE	DAY	SCORE	DAY	SCORE
1		11		21	
2		12		22	
3		13		23	
4		14		24	
5		15		25	
6		16		26	
7		17		27	
8		18		28	
9		19		29	
10		20		30	

NOTES:

OUTSIDE OF THE FOOT DRIBBLING (PULLBACK TURNS)

What You Need To Do This Drill

- A small area of flat ground
- A soccer ball
- 9 markers (boxes, cones, cups)
- This page, a pencil and an eraser

How To Set Up For This Drill

A. Set five markers in a row as shown in the diagram.

B. Set two markers at each end of the row as shown in the diagram.

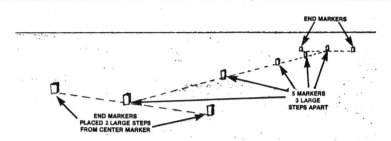

How To Do This Drill

1. Place the ball at your feet near marker 1.

2. Using the outside of both feet dribble the ball around marker 1, 2, 3, 4, and 5. If you hit a marker or the ball goes over the boundary line, start the drill again at marker 1.

3. When you get past marker 5, step on the ball, pull it behind you and turn around.

4. Using the outside of both feet dribble the ball around marker 5, 4, 3, 2, and 1. If you hit a marker or the ball goes over the boundary line, start the drill again at marker 1.

5. If you dribbled the ball from marker 1 through 5 and back without hitting a marker or going out of bounds, give yourself **1 point** in **"Today's Scores."**

6. Do this for 5 minutes.

7. When you have finished count up your points for the day. This is your score.

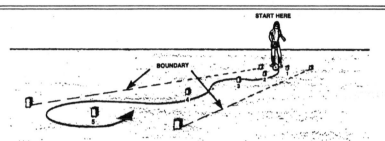

Today's Scores

YOUR GOAL: A score of 5 or more points

	1	2	3	4	5	6	7	8	9	10	11	12	13	14	15	16	17	18	19	20	TOTAL
POINTS																					

How To Watch Your Score Improve

1. Write down your score for today. The first day you do this drill, write your score by **DAY 1**, Write you score for the second day by **DAY 2**, and so on.

2. Did you meet your goal?

NO!

Erase **"Today's Scores"** and do this drill again the next time you **PRACTICE SOCCER BY YOURSELF.**

YES!

WELL DONE! The next time you **PRACTICE SOCCER BY YOURSELF** you can move up to the drill on the next page.

Also cut off the number on the top of this page. Then turn to the **PROGRESS CHART** at the end of the book.

DAY	SCORE	DAY	SCORE	DAY	SCORE
1		11		21	
2		12		22	
3		13		23	
4		14		24	
5		15		25	
6		16		26	
7		17		27	
8		18		28	
9		19		29	
10		20		30	

NOTES:

INSIDE OF THE FOOT DRIBBLING (SQUARE TURNS)

What You Need To Do This Drill

- A small area of flat ground
- A soccer ball
- 9 markers (boxes, cones, cups)
- This page, a pencil and an eraser

How To Set Up For This Drill

A. Set five markers in a row as shown in the diagram.

B. Set two markers at each end of the row as shown in the diagram.

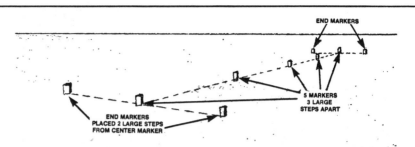

How To Do This Drill

1. Place the ball at your feet near marker 1.

2. Using the inside of both feet dribble the ball around marker 1, 2, 3, 4, and 5. If you hit a marker or the ball goes over the boundary line, start the drill again at marker 1.

3. When you get past marker 5, step over the ball with your right foot, then push the ball behind your right foot with your left foot and turn around.

4. Using the inside of both feet dribble the ball around marker 5, 4, 3, 2, and 1. If you hit a marker or the ball goes over the boundary line, start the drill again at marker 1.

5. If you dribbled the ball from marker 1 through 5 and back without hitting a marker or going out of bounds, give your self **1 point** in **"Today's Scores."**

6. Do this for 5 minutes.

7. When you have finished count up your points for the day. This is your score.

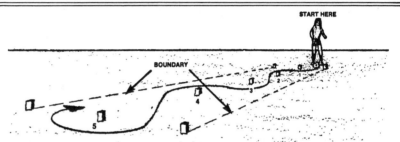

START | LEFT TURN | RIGHT TURN | LEFT TURN

STEP OVER THE BALL

PUSH IT BEHIND YOUR FOOT

Today's Scores

YOUR GOAL: A score of 8 or more points

	1	2	3	4	5	6	7	8	9	10	11	12	13	14	15	16	17	18	19	20	TOTAL
POINTS																					

How To Watch Your Score Improve

1. Write down your score for today. The first day you do this drill, write your score by **DAY 1**, Write you score for the second day by **DAY 2**, and so on.

2. Did you meet your goal?

NO!

Erase **"Today's Scores"** and do this drill again the next time you **PRACTICE SOCCER BY YOURSELF.**

YES!

WELL DONE! The next time you **PRACTICE SOCCER BY YOURSELF** you can move up to the drill on the next page.

Also cut off the number on the top of this page. Then turn to the **PROGRESS CHART** at the end of the book.

DAY	SCORE	DAY	SCORE	DAY	SCORE
1		11		21	
2		12		22	
3		13		23	
4		14		24	
5		15		25	
6		16		26	
7		17		27	
8		18		28	
9		19		29	
10		20		30	

NOTES:

OUTSIDE OF THE FOOT DRIBBLING (SQUARE TURNS)

What You Need To Do This Drill

- A small area of flat ground
- A soccer ball
- 9 markers (boxes, cones, cups)
- This page, a pencil and an eraser

How To Set Up For This Drill

A. Set five markers in a row as shown in the diagram.

B. Set two markers at each end of the row as shown in the diagram.

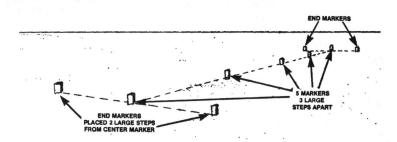

How To Do This Drill

1. Place the ball at your feet near marker 1.

2. Using the outside of both feet dribble the ball around marker 1, 2, 3, 4, and 5. If you hit a marker or the ball goes over the boundary line, start the drill again at marker 1.

3. When you get past marker 5, step over the ball with your left foot, then push the ball behind your left foot with your right foot and turn around.

4. Using the outside of both feet dribble the ball around marker 5, 4, 3, 2, and 1. If you hit a marker or the ball goes over the boundary line, start the drill again at marker 1.

5. If you dribbled the ball from marker 1 through 5 and back without hitting a marker or going out of bounds, give yourself **1 point** in **"Today's Scores."**

6. Do this for 5 minutes.

7. When you have finished count up your points for the day. This is your score.

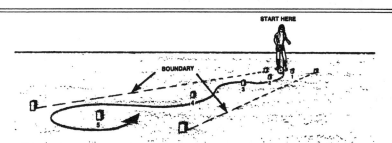

Today's Scores

YOUR GOAL: A score of 5 or more points

	1	2	3	4	5	6	7	8	9	10	11	12	13	14	15	16	17	18	19	20	TOTAL
POINTS																					

How To Watch Your Score Improve

1. Write down your score for today. The first day you do this drill, write your score by **DAY 1**, Write you score for the second day by **DAY 2**, and so on.

2. Did you meet your goal?

NO!

Erase **"Today's Scores"** and do this drill again the next time you **PRACTICE SOCCER BY YOURSELF.**

YES!

WELL DONE! The next time you **PRACTICE SOCCER BY YOURSELF** you can move up to the drill on the next page.

Also cut off the number on the top of this page. Then turn to the **PROGRESS CHART** at the end of the book.

DAY	SCORE
1	
2	
3	
4	
5	
6	
7	
8	
9	
10	

DAY	SCORE
11	
12	
13	
14	
15	
16	
17	
18	
19	
20	

DAY	SCORE
21	
22	
23	
24	
25	
26	
27	
28	
29	
30	

NOTES:

LEFT FOOT DRIBBLING (PULLBACK TURNS)

What You Need To Do This Drill

- A small area of flat ground
- A soccer ball
- 9 markers (boxes, cones, cups)
- This page, a pencil and an eraser

How To Set Up For This Drill

A. Set five markers in a row as shown in the diagram.

B. Set two markers at each end of the row as shown in the diagram.

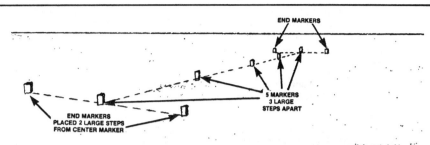

How To Do This Drill

1. Place the ball at your feet near marker 1.

2. Using your left foot only dribble the ball around marker 1, 2, 3, 4, and 5. If you hit a marker or the ball goes over the boundary line, start the drill again at marker 1.

3. When you get past marker 5, step on the ball, pull it behind you and turn around.

4. Using your left foot only dribble the ball around marker 5, 4, 3, 2, and 1. If you hit a marker or the ball goes over the boundary line, start the drill again at marker 1.

5. If you dribbled the ball from marker 1 through 5 and back without hitting a marker or going out of bounds, give yourself **1 point** in **"Today's Scores."**

6. Do this for 5 minutes.

7. When you have finished count up your points for the day. This is your score.

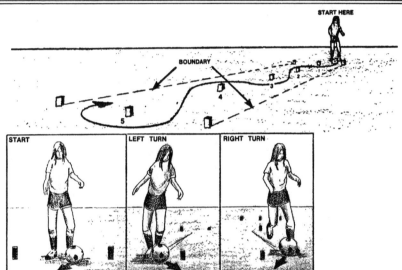

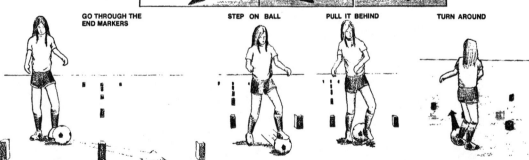

Today's Scores

YOUR GOAL: A score of 8 or more points

	1	2	3	4	5	6	7	8	9	10	11	12	13	14	15	16	17	18	19	20	TOTAL
POINTS																					

How To Watch Your Score Improve

1. Write down your score for today. The first day you do this drill, write your score by **DAY 1**, Write you score for the second day by **DAY 2**, and so on.

2. Did you meet your goal?

NO!

Erase **"Today's Scores"** and do this drill again the next time you **PRACTICE SOCCER BY YOURSELF.**

YES!

WELL DONE! The next time you **PRACTICE SOCCER BY YOURSELF** you can move up to the drill on the next page.

Also cut off the number on the top of this page. Then turn to the **PROGRESS CHART** at the end of the book.

DAY	SCORE
1	
2	
3	
4	
5	
6	
7	
8	
9	
10	

DAY	SCORE
11	
12	
13	
14	
15	
16	
17	
18	
19	
20	

DAY	SCORE
21	
22	
23	
24	
25	
26	
27	
28	
29	
30	

NOTES:

RIGHT FOOT DRIBBLING (HEEL TURNS)

What You Need To Do This Drill

- A small area of flat ground
- A soccer ball
- 9 markers (boxes, cones, cups)
- This page, a pencil and an eraser

How To Set Up For This Drill

A. Set five markers in a row as shown in the diagram.

B. Set two markers at each end of the row as shown in the diagram.

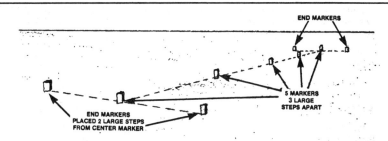

END MARKERS

5 MARKERS
3 LARGE
STEPS APART

END MARKERS
PLACED 2 LARGE STEPS
FROM CENTER MARKER

How To Do This Drill

1. Place the ball at your feet near marker 1.

2. Using your right foot only dribble the ball around marker 1, 2, 3, 4, and 5. If you hit a marker or the ball goes over the boundary line, start the drill again at marker 1.

3. When you get past marker 5, step over the ball, stop it with your heel and turn around.

4. Using your right foot only dribble the ball around marker 5, 4, 3, 2, and 1. If you hit a marker or the ball goes over the boundary line, start the drill again at marker 1.

5. If you dribbled the ball from marker 1 through 5 and back without hitting a marker or going out of bounds, give your self **1 point** in **"Today's Scores."**

6. Do this for 5 minutes.

7. When you have finished count up your points for the day. This is your score.

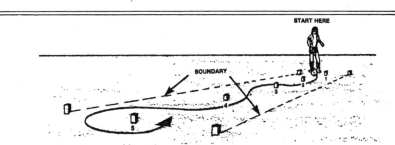

START HERE

BOUNDARY

START | RIGHT TURN | LEFT TURN | RIGHT TURN

GO THROUGH THE END MARKERS | STOP THE BALL WITH YOUR HEEL | TURN AROUND

Today's Scores

YOUR GOAL: A score of 8 or more points

	1	2	3	4	5	6	7	8	9	10	11	12	13	14	15	16	17	18	19	20	TOTAL
POINTS																					

How To Watch Your Score Improve

1. Write down your score for today. The first day you do this drill, write your score by **DAY 1**, Write you score for the second day by **DAY 2**, and so on.

2. Did you meet your goal?

NO!

Erase **"Today's Scores"** and do this drill again the next time you **PRACTICE SOCCER BY YOURSELF.**

YES!

WELL DONE! The next time you **PRACTICE SOCCER BY YOURSELF** you can move up to the drill on the next page.

Also cut off the number on the top of this page. Then turn to the **PROGRESS CHART** at the end of the book.

DAY	SCORE
1	
2	
3	
4	
5	
6	
7	
8	
9	
10	

DAY	SCORE
11	
12	
13	
14	
15	
16	
17	
18	
19	
20	

DAY	SCORE
21	
22	
23	
24	
25	
26	
27	
28	
29	
30	

NOTES:

DRIBBLING (PULLBACK TURNS)

What You Need To Do This Drill

- A small area of flat ground
- A soccer ball
- 9 markers (boxes, cones, cups)
- This page, a pencil and an eraser

How To Set Up For This Drill

A. Set five markers in a row as shown in the diagram.

B. Set two markers at each end of the row as shown in the diagram.

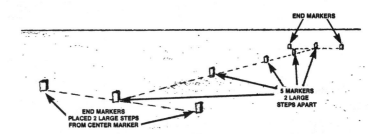

How To Do This Drill

1. Place the ball at your feet near marker 1.

2. Using your feet move (dribble) the ball around marker 1, 2, 3, 4, and 5. If you hit a marker or the ball goes over the boundary line, start the drill again at marker 1.

3. When you get past marker 5, step on the ball, pull it behind you and turn around.

4. Using your feet move (dribble) the ball around marker 5, 4, 3, 2, and 1. If you hit a marker or the ball goes over the boundary line, start the drill again at marker 1.

5. If you dribbled the ball from marker 1 through 5 and back without hitting a marker or going out of bounds, give yourself **1 point** in **"Today's Scores."**

6. Do this for 5 minutes.

7. When you have finished count up your points for the day. This is your score.

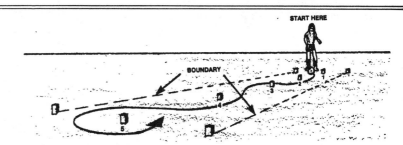

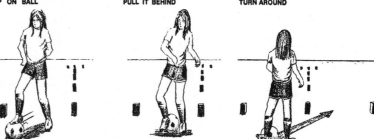

Today's Scores

YOUR GOAL: A score of 8 or more points

	1	2	3	4	5	6	7	8	9	10	11	12	13	14	15	16	17	18	19	20	TOTAL
POINTS																					

How To Watch Your Score Improve

1. Write down your score for today. The first day you do this drill, write your score by **DAY 1**, Write you score for the second day by **DAY 2**, and so on.

2. Did you meet your goal?

NO!

Erase **"Today's Scores"** and do this drill again the next time you **PRACTICE SOCCER BY YOURSELF.**

YES!

WELL DONE! The next time you **PRACTICE SOCCER BY YOURSELF** you can move up to the drill on the next page.

Also cut off the number on the top of this page. Then turn to the **PROGRESS CHART** at the end of the book.

DAY	SCORE	DAY	SCORE	DAY	SCORE
1		11		21	
2		12		22	
3		13		23	
4		14		24	
5		15		25	
6		16		26	
7		17		27	
8		18		28	
9		19		29	
10		20		30	

NOTES:

DRIBBLING (HEEL TURNS)

What You Need To Do This Drill

- A small area of flat ground
- A soccer ball
- 9 markers (boxes, cones, cups)
- This page, a pencil and an eraser

How To Set Up For This Drill

A. Set five markers in a row as shown in the diagram.

B. Set two markers at each end of the row as shown in the diagram.

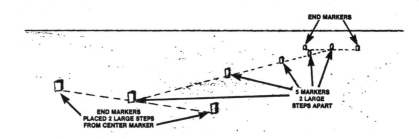

How To Do This Drill

1. Place the ball at your feet near marker 1.

2. Using your feet move (dribble) the ball around marker 1, 2, 3, 4, and 5. If you hit a marker or the ball goes over the boundary line, start the drill again at marker 1.

3. When you get past marker 5, step over the ball, stop it with your heel and turn around.

4. Using your feet move (dribble) the ball around marker 5, 4, 3, 2, and 1. If you hit a marker or the ball goes over the boundary line, start the drill again at marker 1.

5. If you dribbled the ball from marker 1 through 5 and back without hitting a marker or going out of bounds, give yourself **1 point** in **"Today's Scores."**

6. Do this for 5 minutes.

7. When you have finished count up your points for the day. This is your score.

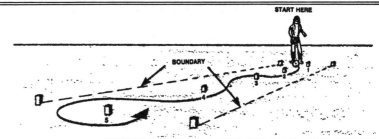

Today's Scores

YOUR GOAL: A score of 8 or more points

	1	2	3	4	5	6	7	8	9	10	11	12	13	14	15	16	17	18	19	20	TOTAL
POINTS																					

How To Watch Your Score Improve

1. Write down your score for today. The first day you do this drill, write your score by **DAY 1**, Write you score for the second day by **DAY 2**, and so on.

2. Did you meet your goal?

NO!

Erase **"Today's Scores"** and do this drill again the next time you **PRACTICE SOCCER BY YOURSELF.**

YES!

WELL DONE! The next time you **PRACTICE SOCCER BY YOURSELF** you can move up to the drill on the next page.

Also cut off the number on the top of this page. Then turn to the **PROGRESS CHART** at the end of the book.

DAY	SCORE		DAY	SCORE		DAY	SCORE
1			11			21	
2			12			22	
3			13			23	
4			14			24	
5			15			25	
6			16			26	
7			17			27	
8			18			28	
9			19			29	
10			20			30	

NOTES:

DRIBBLING (SQUARE TURNS)

What You Need To Do This Drill

- A small area of flat ground
- A soccer ball
- 9 markers (boxes, cones, cups)
- This page, a pencil and an eraser

How To Set Up For This Drill

A. Set five markers in a row as shown in the diagram.

B. Set two markers at each end of the row as shown in the diagram.

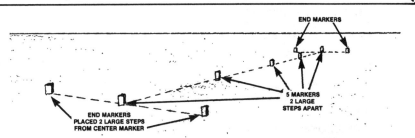

How To Do This Drill

1. Place the ball at your feet near marker 1.

2. Using your feet move (dribble) the ball around marker 1, 2, 3, 4, and 5. If you hit a marker or the ball goes over the boundary line, start the drill again at marker 1.

3. When you get past marker 5, step over the ball with your left foot, then push the ball behind your left foot with your right foot and turn around.

4. Using your feet move (dribble) the ball around marker 5, 4, 3, 2, and 1. If you hit a marker or the ball goes over the boundary line, start the drill again at marker 1.

5. If you dribbled the ball from marker 1 through 5 and back without hitting a marker or going out of bounds, give yourself **1 point** in **"Today's Scores."**

6. Do this for 5 minutes.

7. When you have finished count up your points for the day. This is your score.

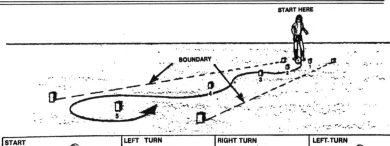

Today's Scores

YOUR GOAL: A score of 8 or more points

	1	2	3	4	5	6	7	8	9	10	11	12	13	14	15	16	17	18	19	20	TOTAL
POINTS																					

How To Watch Your Score Improve

1. Write down your score for today. The first day you do this drill, write your score by **DAY 1**, Write you score for the second day by **DAY 2**, and so on.

2. Did you meet your goal?

NO!

Erase **"Today's Scores"** and do this drill again the next time you **PRACTICE SOCCER BY YOURSELF.**

YES!

WELL DONE! The next time you **PRACTICE SOCCER BY YOURSELF** you can move up to the drill on the next page.

Also cut off the number on the top of this page. Then turn to the **PROGRESS CHART** at the end of the book.

DAY	SCORE
1	
2	
3	
4	
5	
6	
7	
8	
9	
10	

DAY	SCORE
11	
12	
13	
14	
15	
16	
17	
18	
19	
20	

DAY	SCORE
21	
22	
23	
24	
25	
26	
27	
28	
29	
30	

NOTES:

....STOPPING THE BALL

Picture yourself in a soccer game. You are near midfield. The ball is coming to you in the air and none of the other team's players are close to you...

...You look and see that all your teammates are marked* by members of the other team.

Now, think about what you might do.

You could volley kick the ball and hope that a teammate gets it — that's probably not such a good idea.

You could stop the ball and give your teammates time to get away from the players marking them — this is probably a better choice.

Of course you have been practicing your stopping. You stop the ball with your instep, the ball rolls off your foot and stays close to you. You are in good shape to dribble or pass.

Well done!

The following drills will help you learn how to stop the ball with your feet and legs. Also you will learn how to pass the ball quickly after you stop it.

*In soccer when we say "Bill is **marking** Tom" it means that Bill is staying close to Tom to keep him from getting the ball.

INSTEP STOP

What You Need To Do This Drill

- A small area of flat ground
- A soccer ball
- 4 markers (rags, sticks, cans, boxes, cones, etc.)
- This page, a pencil and an eraser

How To Set Up For This Drill

A. Place 4 markers in a square. Each side is 6 large steps long. You must keep the ball inside the square during the drill.

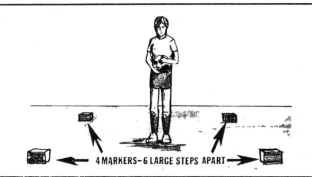

4 MARKERS – 6 LARGE STEPS APART

How To Do This Drill

1. Stand in the middle of the square.

2. Hold the ball in front of you and over your head.

3. Drop the ball.

4. Before the ball touches the ground, stop the ball with the top of either foot (called your instep).

5. Step on the ball before it rolls out of the square.

6. Give yourself **1 point** if you stopped the ball and kept it inside the square. Write down your points in **"Today's Scores."**

7. Do this drill 20 times.

8. After you have done the drill 20 times, add up your points. This is your score.

NOTE: Relax your foot as the ball hits. This will keep the ball from bouncing away from you. Look at the ball as you stop it.

YOUR GOAL: A score of 8 or more points

Today's Scores

	1	2	3	4	5	6	7	8	9	10	11	12	13	14	15	16	17	18	19	20	TOTAL
STOP 1 POINT																					

How To Watch Your Score Improve

1. Write down your score for today. The first day you do this drill, write your score by **DAY 1**, Write you score for the second day by **DAY 2**, and so on.

2. Did you meet your goal?

NO!

Erase **"Today's Scores"** and do this drill again the next time you **PRACTICE SOCCER BY YOURSELF.**

YES!

WELL DONE! The next time you **PRACTICE SOCCER BY YOURSELF** you can move up to the drill on the next page.

Also cut off the number on the top of this page. Then turn to the **PROGRESS CHART** at the end of the book.

DAY	SCORE		DAY	SCORE		DAY	SCORE
1			11			21	
2			12			22	
3			13			23	
4			14			24	
5			15			25	
6			16			26	
7			17			27	
8			18			28	
9			19			29	
10			20			30	

NOTES:

THIGH STOP

What You Need To Do This Drill

- A small area of flat ground
- A soccer ball
- 4 markers (rags, sticks, cans, boxes, cones, etc.)
- This page, a pencil and an eraser

How To Set Up For This Drill

A. Place 4 markers in a square. Each side is 6 large steps long. You must keep the ball inside the square during the drill.

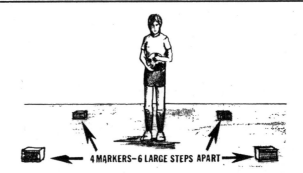

4 MARKERS—6 LARGE STEPS APART

How To Do This Drill

1. Stand in the middle of the square.

2. Hold the ball in front of you and over your head.

3. Drop the ball.

4. Before the ball touches the ground, stop the ball with the top of either leg (called your thigh).

5. Step on the ball before it rolls out of the square.

6. Give yourself **1 point** if you stopped the ball and kept it inside the square. Write down your points in **"Today's Scores."**

7. Do this drill 20 times.

8. After you have done the drill 20 times, add up your points. This is your score.

NOTE: Relax your thigh as the ball hits. This will keep the ball from bouncing away from you. Look at the ball as you stop it.

YOUR GOAL: A score of 8 or more points

Today's Scores

	1	2	3	4	5	6	7	8	9	10	11	12	13	14	15	16	17	18	19	20	TOTAL
STOP 1 POINT																					

How To Watch Your Score Improve

1. Write down your score for today. The first day you do this drill, write your score by **DAY 1**, Write you score for the second day by **DAY 2**, and so on.

2. Did you meet your goal?

NO!

Erase **"Today's Scores"** and do this drill again the next time you **PRACTICE SOCCER BY YOURSELF.**

YES!

WELL DONE! The next time you **PRACTICE SOCCER BY YOURSELF** you can move up to the drill on the next page.

Also cut off the number on the top of this page. Then turn to the **PROGRESS CHART** at the end of the book.

DAY	SCORE		DAY	SCORE		DAY	SCORE
1			11			21	
2			12			22	
3			13			23	
4			14			24	
5			15			25	
6			16			26	
7			17			27	
8			18			28	
9			19			29	
10			20			30	

NOTES:

WEAKER FOOT INSTEP STOP

What You Need To Do This Drill
- A small area of flat ground
- A soccer ball
- 4 markers (rags, sticks, cans, boxes, cones, etc.)
- This page, a pencil and an eraser

How To Set Up For This Drill

A. Place 4 markers in a square. Each side is 6 large steps long. You must keep the ball inside the square during the drill.

4 MARKERS–6 LARGE STEPS APART

How To Do This Drill

1. Stand in the middle of the square.

2. Hold the ball in front of you and over your head.

3. Drop the ball.

4. Before the ball touches the ground, stop the ball with the top of your weaker foot (called your instep).

5. Step on the ball before it rolls out of the square.

6. Give yourself **1 point** if you stopped the ball and kept it inside the square. Write down your points in **"Today's Scores."**

7. Do this drill 20 times.

8. After you have done the drill 20 times, add up your points. This is your score.

NOTE: Your weaker foot is the one you don't usually use to kick the ball. If you are right handed your left foot is likely to be weaker. If you are left handed your right foot is likely to be weaker.

NOTE: Relax your foot as the ball hits. This will keep the ball from bouncing away from you. Look at the ball as you stop it.

Your goal is a score of **4** or more points

Today's Scores

	1	2	3	4	5	6	7	8	9	10	11	12	13	14	15	16	17	18	19	20	TOTAL
STOP 1 POINT																					

How To Watch Your Score Improve

1. Write down your score for today. The first day you do this drill, write your score by **DAY 1**, Write you score for the second day by **DAY 2**, and so on.

2. Did you meet your goal?

NO!

   Erase **"Today's Scores"** and do this drill again the next time you **PRACTICE SOCCER BY YOURSELF.**

YES!

   WELL DONE! The next time you **PRACTICE SOCCER BY YOURSELF** you can move up to the drill on the next page.

   Also cut off the number on the top of this page. Then turn to the **PROGRESS CHART** at the end of the book.

DAY	SCORE		DAY	SCORE		DAY	SCORE
1			11			21	
2			12			22	
3			13			23	
4			14			24	
5			15			25	
6			16			26	
7			17			27	
8			18			28	
9			19			29	
10			20			30	

NOTES:

WEAKER LEG THIGH STOP

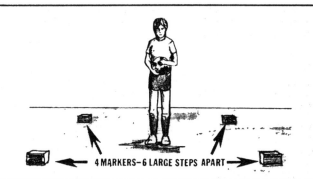

What You Need To Do This Drill

- A small area of flat ground
- A soccer ball
- 4 markers (rags, sticks, cans, boxes, cones, etc.)
- This page, a pencil and an eraser

How To Set Up For This Drill

A. Place 4 markers in a square. Each side is 6 large steps long. You must keep the ball inside the square during the drill.

4 MARKERS–6 LARGE STEPS APART

How To Do This Drill

1. Stand in the middle of the square.

2. Hold the ball in front of you and over your head.

3. Drop the ball.

4. Before the ball touches the ground, stop the ball with the top of your weaker leg (called your thigh).

5. Step on the ball before it rolls out of the square.

6. Give yourself **1 point** if you stopped the ball and kept it inside the square. Write down your points in **"Today's Scores."**

7. Do this drill 20 times.

8. After you have done the drill 20 times, add up your points. This is your score.

NOTE: Your weaker leg is the one you don't usually use to kick the ball. If your are right handed your left leg is likely to be weaker. If your are left handed your right leg is likely to be weaker.

NOTE: Relax your thigh as the ball hits. This will keep the ball from bouncing away from you. Look at the ball as you stop it.

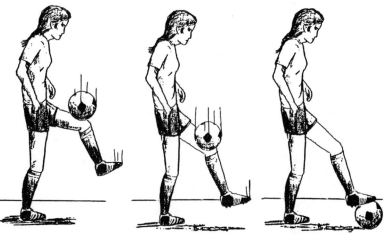

YOUR GOAL: A score of 4 or more points

Today's Scores

	1	2	3	4	5	6	7	8	9	10	11	12	13	14	15	16	17	18	19	20	TOTAL
STOP 1 POINT																					

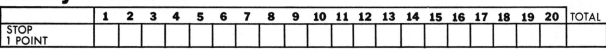

How To Watch Your Score Improve

1. Write down your score for today. The first day you do this drill, write your score by **DAY 1**, Write you score for the second day by **DAY 2**, and so on.

2. Did you meet your goal?

NO!

Erase **"Today's Scores"** and do this drill again the next time you **PRACTICE SOCCER BY YOURSELF.**

YES!

WELL DONE! The next time you **PRACTICE SOCCER BY YOURSELF** you can move up to the drill on the next page.

Also cut off the number on the top of this page. Then turn to the **PROGRESS CHART** at the end of the book.

DAY	SCORE	DAY	SCORE	DAY	SCORE
1		11		21	
2		12		22	
3		13		23	
4		14		24	
5		15		25	
6		16		26	
7		17		27	
8		18		28	
9		19		29	
10		20		30	

NOTES:

LOW THROW, INSTEP STOP

What You Need To Do This Drill

- A small area of flat ground
- A soccer ball
- 4 markers (rags, sticks, cans, boxes, cones, etc.)
- This page, a pencil and an eraser

How To Set Up For This Drill

A. Place 4 markers in a square. Each side is 6 large steps long. You must keep the ball inside the square during the drill.

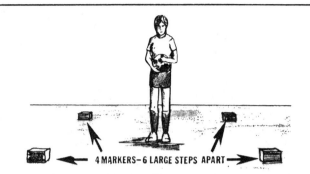

4 MARKERS—6 LARGE STEPS APART

How To Do This Drill

1. Stand in the middle of the square.

2. Hold the ball in front of you.

3. Throw the ball straight up — a little over your head.

4. Before the ball touches the ground, stop the ball with either instep.

5. Step on the ball before it rolls out of the square.

6. Give yourself **1 point** if you stopped the ball and kept it inside the square. Write down your points in **"Today's Scores."**

7. Do this drill 20 times.

8. After you have done the drill 20 times, add up your points. This is your score.

YOUR GOAL: A score of 9 or more points

Today's Scores

	1	2	3	4	5	6	7	8	9	10	11	12	13	14	15	16	17	18	19	20	TOTAL
STOP 1 POINT																					

187

How To Watch Your Score Improve

1. Write down your score for today. The first day you do this drill, write your score by **DAY 1**, Write you score for the second day by **DAY 2**, and so on.

2. Did you meet your goal?

NO!

Erase **"Today's Scores"** and do this drill again the next time you **PRACTICE SOCCER BY YOURSELF.**

YES!

WELL DONE! The next time you **PRACTICE SOCCER BY YOURSELF** you can move up to the drill on the next page.

Also cut off the number on the top of this page. Then turn to the **PROGRESS CHART** at the end of the book.

DAY	SCORE
1	
2	
3	
4	
5	
6	
7	
8	
9	
10	

DAY	SCORE
11	
12	
13	
14	
15	
16	
17	
18	
19	
20	

DAY	SCORE
21	
22	
23	
24	
25	
26	
27	
28	
29	
30	

NOTES:

LOW THROW, WEAKER FOOT

What You Need To Do This Drill

- A small area of flat ground
- A soccer ball
- 4 markers (rags, sticks, cans, boxes, cones, etc.)
- This page, a pencil and an eraser

How To Set Up For This Drill

A. Place 4 markers in a square. Each side is 6 large steps long. You must keep the ball inside the square during the drill.

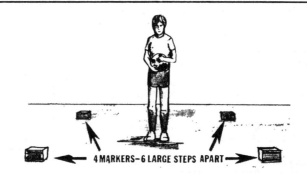

4 MARKERS – 6 LARGE STEPS APART

How To Do This Drill

1. Stand in the middle of the square.

2. Hold the ball in front of you.

3. Throw the ball straight up — a little over your head.

4. Before the ball touches the ground, stop the ball with your weaker instep.

5. Step on the ball before it rolls out of the square.

6. Give yourself **1 point** if you stopped the ball and kept it inside the square. Write down your points in **"Today's Scores."**

7. Do this drill 20 times.

8. After you have done the drill 20 times, add up your points. This is your score.

YOUR GOAL: A score of 5 or more points

Today's Scores

	1	2	3	4	5	6	7	8	9	10	11	12	13	14	15	16	17	18	19	20	TOTAL
STOP 1 POINT																					

How To Watch Your Score Improve

1. Write down your score for today. The first day you do this drill, write your score by **DAY 1,** Write you score for the second day by **DAY 2,** and so on.

2. Did you meet your goal?

NO!

Erase **"Today's Scores"** and do this drill again the next time you **PRACTICE SOCCER BY YOURSELF.**

YES!

WELL DONE! The next time you **PRACTICE SOCCER BY YOURSELF** you can move up to the drill on the next page.

Also cut off the number on the top of this page. Then turn to the **PROGRESS CHART** at the end of the book.

DAY	SCORE	DAY	SCORE	DAY	SCORE
1		11		21	
2		12		22	
3		13		23	
4		14		24	
5		15		25	
6		16		26	
7		17		27	
8		18		28	
9		19		29	
10		20		30	

NOTES:

LOW THROW, THIGH STOP

What You Need To Do This Drill

- A small area of flat ground
- A soccer ball
- 4 markers (rags, sticks, cans, boxes, cones, etc.)
- This page, a pencil and an eraser

How To Set Up For This Drill

A. Place 4 markers in a square. Each side is 6 large steps long. You must keep the ball inside the square during the drill.

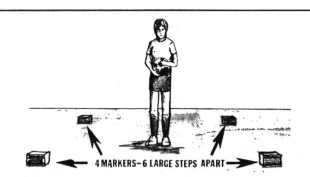

4 MARKERS—6 LARGE STEPS APART

How To Do This Drill

1. Stand in the middle of the square.

2. Hold the ball in front of you.

3. Throw the ball straight up — a little over your head.

4. Before the ball touches the ground, stop the ball with either thigh.

5. Step on the ball before it rolls out of the square.

6. Give yourself **1 point** if you stopped the ball and kept it inside the square. Write down your points in **"Today's Scores."**

7. Do this drill 20 times.

8. After you have done the drill 20 times, add up your points. This is your score.

YOUR GOAL: A score of 9 or more points

Today's Scores

	1	2	3	4	5	6	7	8	9	10	11	12	13	14	15	16	17	18	19	20	TOTAL
STOP 1 POINT																					

How To Watch Your Score Improve

1. Write down your score for today. The first day you do this drill, write your score by **DAY 1**, Write you score for the second day by **DAY 2**, and so on.

2. Did you meet your goal?

NO!

Erase **"Today's Scores"** and do this drill again the next time you **PRACTICE SOCCER BY YOURSELF.**

YES!

WELL DONE! The next time you **PRACTICE SOCCER BY YOURSELF** you can move up to the drill on the next page.

Also cut off the number on the top of this page. Then turn to the **PROGRESS CHART** at the end of the book.

DAY	SCORE	DAY	SCORE	DAY	SCORE
1		11		21	
2		12		22	
3		13		23	
4		14		24	
5		15		25	
6		16		26	
7		17		27	
8		18		28	
9		19		29	
10		20		30	

NOTES:

LOW THROW, WEAKER LEG THIGH STOP

What You Need To Do This Drill

- A small area of flat ground
- A soccer ball
- 4 markers (rags, sticks, cans, boxes, cones, etc.)
- This page, a pencil and an eraser

How To Set Up For This Drill

A. Place 4 markers in a square. Each side is 6 large steps long. You must keep the ball inside the square during the drill.

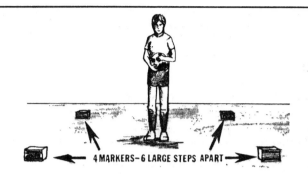

4 MARKERS—6 LARGE STEPS APART

How To Do This Drill

1. Stand in the middle of the square.

2. Hold the ball in front of you.

3. Throw the ball straight up — a little over your head.

4. Before the ball touches the ground, stop the ball with your weaker thigh.

5. Step on the ball before it rolls out of the square.

6. Give yourself **1 point** if you stopped the ball and kept it inside the square. Write down your points in **"Today's Scores."**

7. Do this drill 20 times.

8. After you have done the drill 20 times, add up your points. This is your score.

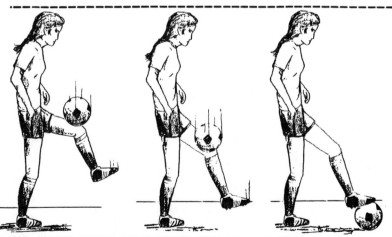

YOUR GOAL: A score of 5 or more points

Today's Scores

	1	2	3	4	5	6	7	8	9	10	11	12	13	14	15	16	17	18	19	20	TOTAL
STOP 1 POINT																					

How To Watch Your Score Improve

1. Write down your score for today. The first day you do this drill, write your score by **DAY 1**, Write you score for the second day by **DAY 2**, and so on.

2. Did you meet your goal?

NO!

Erase **"Today's Scores"** and do this drill again the next time you **PRACTICE SOCCER BY YOURSELF.**

YES!

WELL DONE! The next time you **PRACTICE SOCCER BY YOURSELF** you can move up to the drill on the next page.

Also cut off the number on the top of this page. Then turn to the **PROGRESS CHART** at the end of the book.

DAY	SCORE
1	
2	
3	
4	
5	
6	
7	
8	
9	
10	

DAY	SCORE
11	
12	
13	
14	
15	
16	
17	
18	
19	
20	

DAY	SCORE
21	
22	
23	
24	
25	
26	
27	
28	
29	
30	

NOTES:

HIGH THROW, INSTEP STOP

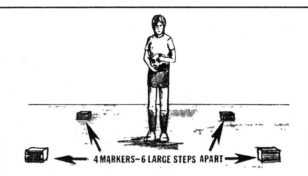

What You Need To Do This Drill

- A small area of flat ground
- A soccer ball
- 4 markers (rags, sticks, cans, boxes, cones, etc.)
- This page, a pencil and an eraser

How To Set Up For This Drill

A. Place 4 markers in a square. Each side is 6 large steps long. You must keep the ball inside the square during the drill.

4 MARKERS–6 LARGE STEPS APART

How To Do This Drill

1. Stand in the middle of the square.

2. Hold the ball in front of you.

3. Throw the ball straight up as high as you can.

4. Before the ball touches the ground, stop the ball with either instep.

5. Step on the ball before it rolls out of the square.

6. Give yourself **1 point** if you stopped the ball and kept it inside the square. Write down your points in **"Today's Scores."**

7. Do this drill 20 times.

8. After you have done the drill 20 times, add up your points. This is your score.

YOUR GOAL: A score of 10 or more points

Today's Scores

	1	2	3	4	5	6	7	8	9	10	11	12	13	14	15	16	17	18	19	20	TOTAL
STOP 1 POINT																					

How To Watch Your Score Improve

1. Write down your score for today. The first day you do this drill, write your score by **DAY 1**, Write you score for the second day by **DAY 2**, and so on.

2. Did you meet your goal?

NO!

Erase **"Today's Scores"** and do this drill again the next time you **PRACTICE SOCCER BY YOURSELF.**

YES!

WELL DONE! The next time you **PRACTICE SOCCER BY YOURSELF** you can move up to the drill on the next page.

Also cut off the number on the top of this page. Then turn to the **PROGRESS CHART** at the end of the book.

DAY	SCORE	DAY	SCORE	DAY	SCORE
1		11		21	
2		12		22	
3		13		23	
4		14		24	
5		15		25	
6		16		26	
7		17		27	
8		18		28	
9		19		29	
10		20		30	

NOTES:

HIGH THROW, WEAKER FOOT INSTEP STOP

What You Need To Do This Drill

- A small area of flat ground
- A soccer ball
- 4 markers (rags, sticks, cans, boxes, cones, etc.)
- This page, a pencil and an eraser

How To Set Up For This Drill

A. Place 4 markers in a square. Each side is 6 large steps long. You must keep the ball inside the square during the drill.

4 MARKERS—6 LARGE STEPS APART

How To Do This Drill

1. Stand in the middle of the square.

2. Hold the ball in front of you.

3. Throw the ball straight up — as high as you can.

4. Before the ball touches the ground, stop the ball with your weaker instep.

5. Step on the ball before it rolls out of the square.

6. Give yourself **1 point** if you stopped the ball and kept it inside the square. Write down your points in **"Today's Scores."**

7. Do this drill 20 times.

8. After you have done the drill 20 times, add up your points. This is your score.

YOUR GOAL: A score of 6 or more points

Today's Scores

	1	2	3	4	5	6	7	8	9	10	11	12	13	14	15	16	17	18	19	20	TOTAL
STOP 1 POINT																					

How To Watch Your Score Improve

1. Write down your score for today. The first day you do this drill, write your score by **DAY 1**, Write you score for the second day by **DAY 2**, and so on.

2. Did you meet your goal?

NO!

Erase **"Today's Scores"** and do this drill again the next time you **PRACTICE SOCCER BY YOURSELF.**

YES!

WELL DONE! The next time you **PRACTICE SOCCER BY YOURSELF** you can move up to the drill on the next page.

Also cut off the number on the top of this page. Then turn to the **PROGRESS CHART** at the end of the book.

DAY	SCORE
1	
2	
3	
4	
5	
6	
7	
8	
9	
10	

DAY	SCORE
11	
12	
13	
14	
15	
16	
17	
18	
19	
20	

DAY	SCORE
21	
22	
23	
24	
25	
26	
27	
28	
29	
30	

NOTES:

HIGH THROW, THIGH STOP

What You Need To Do This Drill

- A small area of flat ground
- A soccer ball
- 4 markers (rags, sticks, cans, boxes, cones, etc.)
- This page, a pencil and an eraser

How To Set Up For This Drill

A. Place 4 markers in a square. Each side is 6 large steps long. You must keep the ball inside the square during the drill.

4 MARKERS—6 LARGE STEPS APART

How To Do This Drill

1. Stand in the middle of the square.

2. Hold the ball in front of you.

3. Throw the ball straight up — as high as you can.

4. Before the ball touches the ground, stop the ball with either thigh.

5. Step on the ball before it rolls out of the square.

6. Give yourself **1 point** if you stopped the ball and kept it inside the square. Write down your points in **"Today's Scores."**

7. Do this drill 20 times.

8. After you have done the drill 20 times, add up your points. This is your score.

YOUR GOAL: A score of 10 or more points

Today's Scores

	1	2	3	4	5	6	7	8	9	10	11	12	13	14	15	16	17	18	19	20	TOTAL
STOP 1 POINT																					

How To Watch Your Score Improve

1. Write down your score for today. The first day you do this drill, write your score by **DAY 1**, Write you score for the second day by **DAY 2**, and so on.

2. Did you meet your goal?

NO!

Erase **"Today's Scores"** and do this drill again the next time you **PRACTICE SOCCER BY YOURSELF.**

YES!

WELL DONE! The next time you **PRACTICE SOCCER BY YOURSELF** you can move up to the drill on the next page.

Also cut off the number on the top of this page. Then turn to the **PROGRESS CHART** at the end of the book.

DAY	SCORE
1	
2	
3	
4	
5	
6	
7	
8	
9	
10	

DAY	SCORE
11	
12	
13	
14	
15	
16	
17	
18	
19	
20	

DAY	SCORE
21	
22	
23	
24	
25	
26	
27	
28	
29	
30	

NOTES:

HIGH THROW, WEAKER LEG THIGH STOP

What You Need To Do This Drill

- A small area of flat ground
- A soccer ball
- 4 markers (rags, sticks, cans, boxes, cones, etc.)
- This page, a pencil and an eraser

How To Set Up For This Drill

A. Place 4 markers in a square. Each side is 6 large steps long. You must keep the ball inside the square during the drill.

4 MARKERS-6 LARGE STEPS APART

How To Do This Drill

1. Stand in the middle of the square.

2. Hold the ball in front of you.

3. Throw the ball straight up — as high as you can.

4. Before the ball touches the ground, stop the ball with your weaker thigh.

5. Step on the ball before it rolls out of the square.

6. Give yourself **1 point** if you stopped the ball and kept it inside the square. Write down your points in **"Today's Scores."**

7. Do this drill 20 times.

8. After you have done the drill 20 times, add up your points. This is your score.

YOUR GOAL: A score of 6 or more points

Today's Scores

	1	2	3	4	5	6	7	8	9	10	11	12	13	14	15	16	17	18	19	20	TOTAL
STOP 1 POINT																					

201

How To Watch Your Score Improve

1. Write down your score for today. The first day you do this drill, write your score by **DAY 1**, Write you score for the second day by **DAY 2**, and so on.

2. Did you meet your goal?

NO!

Erase **"Today's Scores"** and do this drill again the next time you **PRACTICE SOCCER BY YOURSELF.**

YES!

WELL DONE! The next time you **PRACTICE SOCCER BY YOURSELF** you can move up to the drill on the next page.

Also cut off the number on the top of this page. Then turn to the **PROGRESS CHART** at the end of the book.

DAY	SCORE	DAY	SCORE	DAY	SCORE
1		11		21	
2		12		22	
3		13		23	
4		14		24	
5		15		25	
6		16		26	
7		17		27	
8		18		28	
9		19		29	
10		20		30	

NOTES:

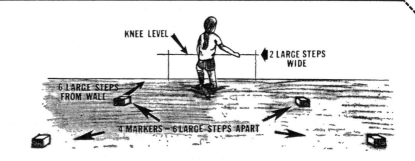

INSTEP STOP, LOW PASS AHEAD

What You Need To Do This Drill

- A small area of flat ground
- A soccer ball
- 4 markers (rags, sticks, cans, boxes, cones, etc.)
- This page, a pencil and an eraser

How To Set Up For This Drill

A. Place markers in a square 6 large steps from the wall. Each side of the square is 6 large steps long. During this drill you must kick the ball before it rolls out of the square.

B. Draw a target on the wall 2 large steps long and as high as your knees. You must hit this target with your pass.

How To Do This Drill

1. Stand in the middle of the square facing the wall.

2. Throw the ball straight up as high as you can.

3. Before the ball touches the ground, stop the ball with the instep of either foot.

4. Before the ball rolls out of the square, kick the ball at the target on the wall.

5. Give yourself **1 point** if you stopped the ball with your instep and kicked it before it rolled out of the square. Give yourself **1 point** if you hit the target. Write down your points in **"Today's Scores."**

6. Do this drill 20 times.

7. After you have done the drill 20 times, add up your points. This is your score.

> **NOTE:** To kick the ball low, bend your body forward over the ball.
>
> **NOTE:** To kick the ball low, kick it at or above its center point.
>
> **NOTE:** Kick the ball with the inside of your foot. This type of kick will help you kick the ball where you want it to go.

YOUR GOAL: A score of 15 or more points

Today's Scores

	1	2	3	4	5	6	7	8	9	10	11	12	13	14	15	16	17	18	19	20	TOTAL
STOPS 1 POINT																					
HIT THE TARGET 1 POINT																					

How To Watch Your Score Improve

1. Write down your score for today. The first day you do this drill, write your score by **DAY 1**, Write you score for the second day by **DAY 2**, and so on.

2. Did you meet your goal?

NO!

Erase **"Today's Scores"** and do this drill again the next time you **PRACTICE SOCCER BY YOURSELF**.

YES!

WELL DONE! The next time you **PRACTICE SOCCER BY YOURSELF** you can move up to the drill on the next page.

Also cut off the number on the top of this page. Then turn to the **PROGRESS CHART** at the end of the book.

DAY	SCORE	DAY	SCORE	DAY	SCORE
1		11		21	
2		12		22	
3		13		23	
4		14		24	
5		15		25	
6		16		26	
7		17		27	
8		18		28	
9		19		29	
10		20		30	

NOTES:

WEAKER FOOT INSTEP STOP, LOW PASS AHEAD

What You Need To Do This Drill

- A small area of flat ground
- A soccer ball
- 4 markers (rags, sticks, cans, boxes, cones, etc.)
- This page, a pencil and an eraser

How To Set Up For This Drill

A. Place markers in a square 6 large steps from the wall. Each side of the square is 6 large steps long. During this drill you must kick the ball before it rolls out of the square.

B. Draw a target on the wall 2 large steps long and as high as your knees. You must hit this target with your pass.

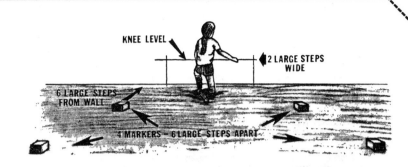

How To Do This Drill

1. Stand in the middle of the square facing the wall.

2. Throw the ball straight up as high as you can.

3. Before the ball touches the ground, stop it with the instep of your weaker foot.

4. Before the ball rolls out of the square, kick the ball at the target on the wall.

5. Give yourself **1 point** if you stopped the ball with your instep and kicked it before it rolled out of the square. Give yourself **1 point** if you hit the target. Write down your points in **"Today's Scores."**

6. Do this drill 20 times.

7. After you have done the drill 20 times, add up your points. This is your score.

NOTE: Look at the target, then look down at the ball as you kick it.

NOTE: To kick the ball low, bend your body forward over the ball.

NOTE: To kick the ball low, kick it at or above its center point.

NOTE: Kick the ball with the inside of your foot. This type of kick will help you kick the ball where you want it to go.

YOUR GOAL: A score of 9 or more points

Today's Scores

	1	2	3	4	5	6	7	8	9	10	11	12	13	14	15	16	17	18	19	20	TOTAL
STOPS 1 POINT																					
HIT THE TARGET 1 POINT																					

How To Watch Your Score Improve

1. Write down your score for today. The first day you do this drill, write your score by **DAY 1**, Write you score for the second day by **DAY 2**, and so on.

2. Did you meet your goal?

NO!

Erase **"Today's Scores"** and do this drill again the next time you **PRACTICE SOCCER BY YOURSELF.**

YES!

WELL DONE! The next time you **PRACTICE SOCCER BY YOURSELF** you can move up to the drill on the next page.

Also cut off the number on the top of this page. Then turn to the **PROGRESS CHART** at the end of the book.

DAY	SCORE
1	
2	
3	
4	
5	
6	
7	
8	
9	
10	

DAY	SCORE
11	
12	
13	
14	
15	
16	
17	
18	
19	
20	

DAY	SCORE
21	
22	
23	
24	
25	
26	
27	
28	
29	
30	

NOTES:

THIGH STOP, LOW PASS AHEAD

What You Need To Do This Drill

- A small area of flat ground
- A soccer ball
- 4 markers (rags, sticks, cans, boxes, cones, etc.)
- This page, a pencil and an eraser

How To Set Up For This Drill

A. Place markers in a square 6 large steps from the wall. Each side of the square is 6 large steps long. During this drill you must kick the ball before it rolls out of the square.

B. Draw a target on the wall 2 large steps long and as high as your knees. You must hit this target with your pass.

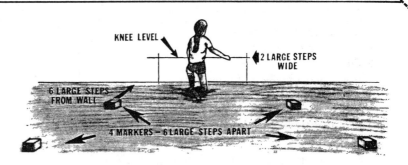

How To Do This Drill

1. Stand in the middle of the square facing the wall.

2. Throw the ball straight up as high as you can.

3. Before the ball touches the ground, stop it with the thigh of either leg.

4. Before the ball rolls out of the square, kick the ball at the target on the wall.

5. Give yourself **1 point** if you stopped the ball with your thigh and kicked it before it rolled out of the square.Give yourself **1 point** if you hit the target. Write down your points in **"Today's Scores."**

6. Do this drill 20 times.

7. After you have done the drill 20 times, add up your points. This is your score.

YOUR GOAL: A score of 18 or more points

Today's Scores

	1	2	3	4	5	6	7	8	9	10	11	12	13	14	15	16	17	18	19	20	TOTAL
STOP 1 POINT																					
HIT THE TARGET 1 POINT																					

How To Watch Your Score Improve

1. Write down your score for today. The first day you do this drill, write your score by **DAY 1**, Write you score for the second day by **DAY 2**, and so on.

2. Did you meet your goal?

NO!

Erase **"Today's Scores"** and do this drill again the next time you **PRACTICE SOCCER BY YOURSELF.**

YES!

WELL DONE! The next time you **PRACTICE SOCCER BY YOURSELF** you can move up to the drill on the next page.

Also cut off the number on the top of this page. Then turn to the **PROGRESS CHART** at the end of the book.

DAY	SCORE
1	
2	
3	
4	
5	
6	
7	
8	
9	
10	

DAY	SCORE
11	
12	
13	
14	
15	
16	
17	
18	
19	
20	

DAY	SCORE
21	
22	
23	
24	
25	
26	
27	
28	
29	
30	

NOTES:

WEAKER THIGH STOP, LOW PASS AHEAD

What You Need To Do This Drill

- A small area of flat ground
- A soccer ball
- 4 markers (rags, sticks, cans, boxes, cones, etc.)
- This page, a pencil and an eraser

How to Set Up For This Drill

A. Place markers in a square 6 large steps from the wall. Each side of the square is 6 large steps long. During this drill you must kick the ball before it rolls out of the square.

B. Draw a target on the wall 2 large steps long and as high as your knees. You must hit this target with your pass.

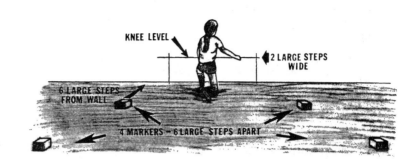

KNEE LEVEL

2 LARGE STEPS WIDE

6 LARGE STEPS FROM WALL

4 MARKERS – 6 LARGE STEPS APART

How To Do This Drill

1. Stand in the middle of the square facing the wall.

2. Throw the ball straight up as high as you can.

3. Before the ball touches the ground, stop it with your weaker thigh of either leg.

4. Before the ball rolls out of the square, kick the ball at the target on the wall.

5. Give yourself **1 point** if you stopped the ball with your thigh and kicked it before it rolled out of the square. Give yourself **1 point** if your hit the target. Write down your points in **"Today's Scores"**.

6. Do this drill 20 times.

7. After you have done the drill 20 times, add up your points. This is your score.

YOUR GOAL: A score of 12 or more points

Today's Scores

	1	2	3	4	5	6	7	8	9	10	11	12	13	14	15	16	17	18	19	20	TOTAL
STOPS 1 POINT																					
HIT THE TARGET 1 POINT																					

How To Watch Your Score Improve

1. Write down your score for today. The first day you do this drill, write your score by **DAY 1**, Write you score for the second day by **DAY 2**, and so on.

2. Did you meet your goal?

NO!

Erase **"Today's Scores"** and do this drill again the next time you **PRACTICE SOCCER BY YOURSELF.**

YES!

WELL DONE! The next time you **PRACTICE SOCCER BY YOURSELF** you can move up to the drill on the next page.

Also cut off the number on the top of this page. Then turn to the **PROGRESS CHART** at the end of the book.

DAY	SCORE
1	
2	
3	
4	
5	
6	
7	
8	
9	
10	

DAY	SCORE
11	
12	
13	
14	
15	
16	
17	
18	
19	
20	

DAY	SCORE
21	
22	
23	
24	
25	
26	
27	
28	
29	
30	

NOTES:

INSTEP STOP, HIGH PASS AHEAD

What You Need To Do This Drill

- A small area of flat ground
- A soccer ball
- 4 markers (rags, sticks, cans, boxes, cones, etc.)
- This page, a pencil and an eraser

How To Set Up For This Drill

A. Place markers in a square 6 large steps from the wall. Each side of the square is 6 large steps long. During this drill you must kick the ball before it rolls out of the square.

B. Draw a line on the wall 2 large steps long and as high as the top of your head. You must kick the ball over this line.

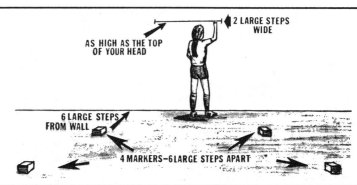

AS HIGH AS THE TOP OF YOUR HEAD

2 LARGE STEPS WIDE

6 LARGE STEPS FROM WALL

4 MARKERS—6 LARGE STEPS APART

How To Do This Drill

1. Stand in the middle of the square facing the wall.

2. Throw the ball straight up as high as you can.

3. Before the ball touches the ground, stop the ball with the instep of either foot.

4. Before the ball rolls out of the square, kick the ball over the line on the wall.

5. Give yourself **1 point** if you stopped the ball with your instep and kicked it before it rolled out of the square. Give yourself **1 point** if you kicked the ball over the line on the wall. Write down your points in **"Today's Scores."**

6. Do this drill 20 times.

7. After you have done the drill 20 times, add up your points. This is your score.

> **NOTE:** Kick the ball with your instep. This type of kick is for power and distance.

> **NOTE:** Look at the target, then look down at the ball as you kick it.

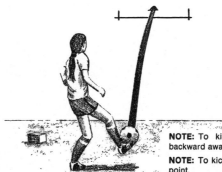

> **NOTE:** To kick the ball high, bend your body backward away from the ball.

> **NOTE:** To kick the ball high, kick it below its center point.

YOUR GOAL: A score of 21 or more points

Today's Scores

	1	2	3	4	5	6	7	8	9	10	11	12	13	14	15	16	17	18	19	20	TOTAL
STOPS 1 POINT																					
HIT THE TARGET 1 POINT																					

How To Watch Your Score Improve

1. Write down your score for today. The first day you do this drill, write your score by **DAY 1**, Write you score for the second day by **DAY 2**, and so on.

2. Did you meet your goal?

NO!

Erase **"Today's Scores"** and do this drill again the next time you **PRACTICE SOCCER BY YOURSELF.**

YES!

WELL DONE! The next time you **PRACTICE SOCCER BY YOURSELF** you can move up to the drill on the next page.

Also cut off the number on the top of this page. Then turn to the **PROGRESS CHART** at the end of the book.

DAY	SCORE
1	
2	
3	
4	
5	
6	
7	
8	
9	
10	

DAY	SCORE
11	
12	
13	
14	
15	
16	
17	
18	
19	
20	

DAY	SCORE
21	
22	
23	
24	
25	
26	
27	
28	
29	
30	

NOTES:

WEAKER FOOT INSTEP STOP, HIGH PASS AHEAD

What You Need To Do This Drill

- A small area of flat ground
- A soccer ball
- 4 markers (rags, sticks, cans, boxes, cones, etc.)
- This page, a pencil and an eraser

How To Set Up For This Drill

A. Place markers in a square 6 large steps from the wall. Each side of the square is 6 large steps long. During this drill you must kick the ball before it rolls out of the square.

B. Draw a line on the wall 2 large steps long and as high as the top of your head. You must kick the ball over this line.

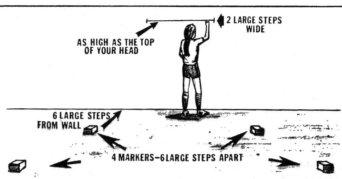

AS HIGH AS THE TOP OF YOUR HEAD

2 LARGE STEPS WIDE

6 LARGE STEPS FROM WALL

4 MARKERS—6 LARGE STEPS APART

How To Do This Drill

1. Stand in the middle of the square facing the wall.

2. Throw the ball straight up as high as you can.

3. Before the ball touches the ground, stop it with the instep of your weaker foot.

4. Before the ball rolls out of the square, kick the ball over the line on the wall.

5. Give yourself **1 point** if you stopped the ball with your weaker instep and kicked it before it rolled out of the square. Give yourself **1 point** if you kicked the ball over the line on the wall. Write down your points in **"Today's Scores."**

6. Do this drill 20 times.

7. After you have done the drill 20 times, add up your points. This is your score.

NOTE: To kick the ball high, bend your body backward away from the ball.

NOTE: To kick the ball high, kick it below its center point.

NOTE: Look at the target, then look down at the ball as you kick it.

NOTE: Kick the ball with your instep. This type of kick is for power and distance.

YOUR GOAL: A score of 15 or more points

Today's Scores

	1	2	3	4	5	6	7	8	9	10	11	12	13	14	15	16	17	18	19	20	TOTAL
STOP 1 POINT																					
HIT THE TARGET 1 POINT																					

How To Watch Your Score Improve

1. Write down your score for today. The first day you do this drill, write your score by **DAY 1**, Write you score for the second day by **DAY 2**, and so on.

2. Did you meet your goal?

NO!

Erase **"Today's Scores"** and do this drill again the next time you **PRACTICE SOCCER BY YOURSELF.**

YES!

WELL DONE! The next time you **PRACTICE SOCCER BY YOURSELF** you can move up to the drill on the next page.

Also cut off the number on the top of this page. Then turn to the **PROGRESS CHART** at the end of the book.

DAY	SCORE	DAY	SCORE	DAY	SCORE
1		11		21	
2		12		22	
3		13		23	
4		14		24	
5		15		25	
6		16		26	
7		17		27	
8		18		28	
9		19		29	
10		20		30	

NOTES:

THIGH STOP, HIGH PASS AHEAD

What You Need To Do This Drill

- A small area of flat ground
- A soccer ball
- 4 markers (rags, sticks, cans, boxes, cones, etc.)
- This page, a pencil and an eraser

How To Set Up For This Drill

A. Place markers in a square 6 large steps from the wall. Each side of the square is 6 large steps long. During this drill you must kick the ball before it rolls out of the square.

B. Draw a line on the wall 2 large steps long and as high as the top of your head. You must kick the ball over this line.

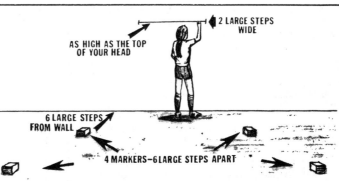

How To Do This Drill

1. Stand in the middle of the square facing the wall.

2. Throw the ball straight up as high as you can.

3. Before the ball touches the ground, stop it with the thigh of either leg.

4. Before the ball rolls out of the square, kick the ball over the line on the wall.

5. Give yourself **1 point** if you stopped the ball with your thigh and kicked it before it rolled out of the square. Give yourself **1 point** if you kicked it over the line on the wall. Write down your points in **"Today's Scores."**

6. Do this drill 20 times.

   NOTE: Kick the ball with your instep. This type of kick is for power and distance.

   NOTE: Look at the target, then look down at the ball as you kick it.

NOTE: To kick the ball high, bend your body backward away from the ball.

NOTE: To kick the ball high, kick it below its center point.

YOUR GOAL: A score of 24 or more stops

Today's Scores

	1	2	3	4	5	6	7	8	9	10	11	12	13	14	15	16	17	18	19	20	TOTAL
STOPS 1 POINT																					
HIT THE TARGET 1 POINT																					

How To Watch Your Score Improve

1. Write down your score for today. The first day you do this drill, write your score by **DAY 1**, Write you score for the second day by **DAY 2**, and so on.

2. Did you meet your goal?

NO!

Erase **"Today's Scores"** and do this drill again the next time you **PRACTICE SOCCER BY YOURSELF.**

YES!

WELL DONE! The next time you **PRACTICE SOCCER BY YOURSELF** you can move up to the drill on the next page.

Also cut off the number on the top of this page. Then turn to the **PROGRESS CHART** at the end of the book.

DAY	SCORE	DAY	SCORE	DAY	SCORE
1		11		21	
2		12		22	
3		13		23	
4		14		24	
5		15		25	
6		16		26	
7		17		27	
8		18		28	
9		19		29	
10		20		30	

NOTES:

WEAKER LEG THIGH STOP, HIGH PASS AHEAD

What You Need To Do This Drill

- A small area of flat ground
- A soccer ball
- 4 markers (rags, sticks, cans, boxes, cones, etc.)
- This page, a pencil and an eraser

How To Set Up For This Drill

A. Place markers in a square 6 large steps from the wall. Each side of the square is 6 large steps long. During this drill you must kick the ball before it rolls out of the square.

B. Draw a line on the wall 2 large steps long and as high as the top of your head. You must kick the ball over this line.

AS HIGH AS THE TOP OF YOUR HEAD

2 LARGE STEPS WIDE

6 LARGE STEPS FROM WALL

4 MARKERS—6 LARGE STEPS APART

How To Do This Drill

1. Stand in the middle of the square facing the wall.

2. Throw the ball straight up as high as you can.

3. Before the ball touches the ground, stop it with the thigh of either weaker leg.

4. Before the ball rolls out of the square, kick the ball over the line on the wall.

5. Give yourself **1 point** if you stopped the ball with your thigh and kicked it before it rolled out of the square. Give yourself **1 point** if you kicked the ball over the line on the wall. Write down your points in **"Today's Scores."**

6. Do this drill 20 times.

7. After you have done the drill 20 times, add up your points. This is your score.

YOUR GOAL: A score of 18 or more points

Today's Scores

	1	2	3	4	5	6	7	8	9	10	11	12	13	14	15	16	17	18	19	20	TOTAL
STOPS 1 POINT																					
HIT THE TARGET 1 POINT																					

How To Watch Your Score Improve

1. Write down your score for today. The first day you do this drill, write your score by **DAY 1**, Write you score for the second day by **DAY 2**, and so on.

2. Did you meet your goal?

NO!

Erase **"Today's Scores"** and do this drill again the next time you **PRACTICE SOCCER BY YOURSELF.**

YES!

WELL DONE! The next time you **PRACTICE SOCCER BY YOURSELF** you can move up to the drill on the next page.

Also cut off the number on the top of this page. Then turn to the **PROGRESS CHART** at the end of the book.

DAY	SCORE	DAY	SCORE	DAY	SCORE
1		11		21	
2		12		22	
3		13		23	
4		14		24	
5		15		25	
6		16		26	
7		17		27	
8		18		28	
9		19		29	
10		20		30	

NOTES:

Why Should You Practice...

Picture yourself in a soccer game. One of your teammates passes the ball to you. As you prepare to stop the ball you see another teammate running into good position to shoot a goal.

You also see a player from the other team moving in to take the ball away from you.

Now, think about what you might do. If you pass the ball quickly and well, your teammate will be able to shoot. Otherwise you will have to keep the other team's player from getting the ball.

You have been working hard on your rebounds, so when the ball gets to you, you stop it quickly and pass to your teammate.

Well done!

During a game the ball usually comes to you on the ground or on a low bounce. You must be able to pass the ball quickly and well. Good passing is the most important skill in soccer.

...REBOUNDING?

The following drills teach you two types of passing.

1. **ONE-TOUCH PASSING** — Where you pass the ball without stopping it first. This pass is used when players from the other team are very close to you.

2. **TWO-TOUCH PASSING** — When player from the other team are not too close to you, you may want to stop the ball (with one touch) and than pass the ball (with the second touch). You will get more accurate passes with two touches. Be careful, though, the second touch can give the other team's player time to move in and try to take the ball.

TWO TOUCH REBOUNDING AT A LARGE TARGET

What You Need To Do This Drill

- A small area of flat ground with a wall at one end
- A soccer ball
- Two markers (sticks, cans, rags, etc.)
- This page, a pencil and an eraser

How to Set Up For This Drill

A. Draw a target on the wall. The target is two large steps wide and goes from the ground to as high as you can reach.

B. Set up the markers 5 large steps from the wall and 8 large steps apart.

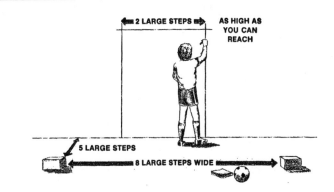

How To Do This Drill

1. Place the ball on the ground in front of the target and further from the wall than the markers.

2. Kick the ball at the target on the wall.

3. When the ball bounces off the target, stop the ball with your leg or foot or body. Don't go closer to the wall than the markers.

4. Kick the ball at the target. Don't go closer to the wall than the markers.

5. Every time the ball bounces off the target, stop the ball with your leg or foot or body. Then kick the ball at the target.

6. Count the number of times in a row you hit the target. This is your score.

7. When you miss the target or don't stop the ball: stop the drill; write down your score in **"Today's Scores;"** Then start again at **step 1.**

8. Do this drill for 5 minutes.

NOTE: Look at the target, then look down at the ball as you kick it.

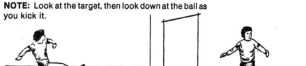

NOTE: Kick the ball with the inside of your foot. This type of kick will help you kick the ball where you want it to go.

NOTE: To stop the ball you can use the inside, outside, top, or bottom of your foot, or you can use your shins, thighs, stomach, chest or head.
NOTE: Relax your foot or leg as the ball hits it. This will help to keep the ball near you so you can kick it quickly.

Today's Scores

YOUR GOAL: A score of 5 or more hits

	1	2	3	4	5	6	7	8	9	10	11	12	13	14	15	16	17	18	19	20
NUMBER OF HITS																				

How To Watch Your Score Improve

1. Write down your score for today. The first day you do this drill, write your score by **DAY 1**, Write you score for the second day by **DAY 2**, and so on.

2. Did you meet your goal?

NO!

Erase **"Today's Scores"** and do this drill again the next time you **PRACTICE SOCCER BY YOURSELF.**

YES!

WELL DONE! The next time you **PRACTICE SOCCER BY YOURSELF** you can move up to the drill on the next page.

Also cut off the number on the top of this page. Then turn to the **PROGRESS CHART** at the end of the book.

DAY	SCORE
1	
2	
3	
4	
5	
6	
7	
8	
9	
10	

DAY	SCORE
11	
12	
13	
14	
15	
16	
17	
18	
19	
20	

DAY	SCORE
21	
22	
23	
24	
25	
26	
27	
28	
29	
30	

NOTES:

WEAK SIDE STOP, TWO-TOUCH REBOUNDING AT A LARGE TARGET

What You Need To Do This Drill

- A small area of flat ground with a wall at one end
- A soccer ball
- Two markers (sticks, cans, rags, etc.)
- This page, a pencil and an eraser

How to Set Up For This Drill

A. Draw a target on the wall. The target is two large steps wide and goes from the ground to as high as you can reach.

B. Set up the markers 5 large steps from the wall and 8 large steps apart.

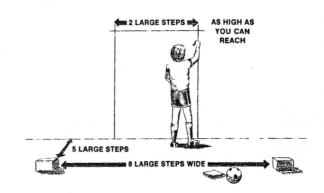

2 LARGE STEPS — AS HIGH AS YOU CAN REACH

5 LARGE STEPS

8 LARGE STEPS WIDE

How To Do This Drill

1. Place the ball on the ground in front of the target and further from the wall than the markers.

2. Kick the ball at the target on the wall.

3. When the ball bounces off the target, stop the ball with your weaker leg or foot. Don't go closer to the wall than the markers.

4. Kick the ball at the target. Don't go closer to the wall than the markers.

5. Every time the ball bounces off the target, stop the ball with your weaker leg or foot. Then kick the ball at the target .

6. Count the number of times in a row you hit the target. This is your score.

7. When you miss the target or don't stop the ball: stop the drill; write down your score in **"Today's Scores."** Then start again at **step 1.**

8. Do this drill for 5 minutes.

NOTE: Look at the target, then look down at the ball as you kick it.

NOTE: Kick the ball with the inside of your foot. This type of kick will help you kick the ball where you want it to

NOTE: Your weaker foot is the one you don't usually use to kick the ball. If you are right handed your left foot is likely to be weaker. If you are left handed your right foot is likely to be weaker.

Today's Scores

YOUR GOAL: A score of 5 or more hits

	1	2	3	4	5	6	7	8	9	10	11	12	13	14	15	16	17	18	19	20
NUMBER OF HITS																				

How To Watch Your Score Improve

1. Write down your score for today. The first day you do this drill, write your score by **DAY 1**, Write you score for the second day by **DAY 2**, and so on.

2. Did you meet your goal?

NO!

Erase **"Today's Scores"** and do this drill again the next time you **PRACTICE SOCCER BY YOURSELF.**

YES!

WELL DONE! The next time you **PRACTICE SOCCER BY YOURSELF** you can move up to the drill on the next page.

Also cut off the number on the top of this page. Then turn to the **PROGRESS CHART** at the end of the book.

DAY	SCORE		DAY	SCORE		DAY	SCORE
1			11			21	
2			12			22	
3			13			23	
4			14			24	
5			15			25	
6			16			26	
7			17			27	
8			18			28	
9			19			29	
10			20			30	

NOTES:

ONE-TOUCH REBOUNDING AT A LARGE TARGET

What You Need To Do This Drill

- A small area of flat ground with a wall at one end
- A soccer ball
- Two markers (sticks, cans, rags, etc.)
- This page, a pencil and an eraser

How to Set Up For This Drill

A. Draw a target on the wall. The target is two large steps wide and goes from the ground to as high as you can reach.

B. Set up the markers 5 large steps from the wall and 8 large steps apart.

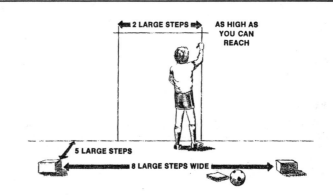

How To Do This Drill

1. Place the ball on the ground in front of the target and further from the wall than the markers.

2. Kick the ball at the target on the wall.

3. When the ball bounces off the target, kick the ball at the target. Don't go closer to the wall than the markers, and DON'T STOP THE BALL BEFORE YOU KICK IT.

4. Every time the ball bounces off the target, kick the ball at the target.

5. Count the number of times in a row you hit the target. This is your score.

7. When you miss the target: stop the drill; write down your score in **"Today's Scores."** Then start again at step 1.

8. Do this drill for 5 minutes.

NOTE: Look at the target, then look down at the ball as you kick it.

NOTE: Kick the ball with the inside of your foot. This type of kick will help you kick the ball where you want it to go.

Today's Scores

YOUR GOAL: A score of 5 or more hits

	1	2	3	4	5	6	7	8	9	10	11	12	13	14	15	16	17	18	19	20
NUMBER OF HITS																				

How To Watch Your Score Improve

1. Write down your score for today. The first day you do this drill, write your score by **DAY 1**, Write you score for the second day by **DAY 2**, and so on.

2. Did you meet your goal?

NO!

Erase **"Today's Scores"** and do this drill again the next time you **PRACTICE SOCCER BY YOURSELF.**

YES!

WELL DONE! The next time you **PRACTICE SOCCER BY YOURSELF** you can move up to the drill on the next page.

Also cut off the number on the top of this page. Then turn to the **PROGRESS CHART** at the end of the book.

DAY	SCORE	DAY	SCORE	DAY	SCORE
1		11		21	
2		12		22	
3		13		23	
4		14		24	
5		15		25	
6		16		26	
7		17		27	
8		18		28	
9		19		29	
10		20		30	

NOTES:

WEAK FOOT KICK,
ONE-TOUCH REBOUNDING AT A LARGE TARGET

What You Need To Do This Drill

- A small area of flat ground with a wall at one end
- A soccer ball
- Two markers (sticks, cans, rags, etc.)
- This page, a pencil and an eraser

How to Set Up For This Drill

A. Draw a target on the wall. The target is two large steps wide and goes from the ground to as high as you can reach.

B. Set up the markers 5 large steps from the wall and 8 large steps apart.

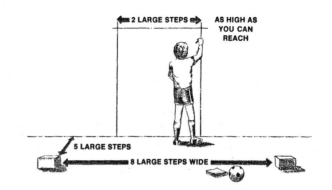

How To Do This Drill

1. Place the ball on the ground in front of the target and further from the wall than the markers.

2. Kick the ball at the target on the wall with your weaker foot.

3. When the ball bounces off the target, kick the ball at the target. Don't go closer to the wall than the markers and DON'T STOP THE BALL BEFORE YOU KICK IT.

4. Every time the ball bounces off the target, kick the ball at the target with your weaker foot.

5. Count the number of times in a row you hit the target. This is your score.

7. When you miss the target: stop the drill; write down your score in **"Today's Scores."** Then start again at **step 1.**

8. Do this drill for 5 minutes.

NOTE: Your weaker foot is the one you don't usually use to kick the ball. If you are right handed your left foot is likely to be weaker. If you are left handed your right foot is likely to be weaker.

NOTE: Look at the target, then look down at the ball as you kick it.

NOTE: Kick the ball with the inside of your foot. This type of kick will help you kick the ball where you want it to go.

Today's Scores

YOUR GOAL: A score of 4 or more hits

	1	2	3	4	5	6	7	8	9	10	11	12	13	14	15	16	17	18	19	20
NUMBER OF HITS																				

How To Watch Your Score Improve

1. Write down your score for today. The first day you do this drill, write your score by **DAY 1**, Write you score for the second day by **DAY 2**, and so on.

2. Did you meet your goal?

NO!

Erase **"Today's Scores"** and do this drill again the next time you **PRACTICE SOCCER BY YOURSELF.**

YES!

WELL DONE! The next time you **PRACTICE SOCCER BY YOURSELF** you can move up to the drill on the next page.

Also cut off the number on the top of this page. Then turn to the **PROGRESS CHART** at the end of the book.

DAY	SCORE	DAY	SCORE	DAY	SCORE
1		11		21	
2		12		22	
3		13		23	
4		14		24	
5		15		25	
6		16		26	
7		17		27	
8		18		28	
9		19		29	
10		20		30	

NOTES:

HEAD CLEAR REBOUNDING

What You Need To Do This Drill
- A small area of flat ground with a wall at one end
- A soccer ball
- This page, a pencil and an eraser

How to Set Up For This Drill
A. No set up is needed

How To Do This Drill

1. Stand about three steps out from the wall, holding the ball and facing the wall.

2. Throw the ball high up on the wall.

3. When it bounces off the wall, hit the ball back up on the wall with your forehead. Don't let the ball touch the ground.

4. Every time the ball bounces off the wall, head the ball back up on the wall.

5. Count the number of times in a row you hit the ball up on the wall with your head before the ball drops to the ground. This is your score.

6. When the ball drops to the ground; stop the drill; write down your score in **"Todays Scores."** then start again at **step 1.**

7. Do this drill for 5 minutes.

NOTE: When you hit the ball with your head:
  a. be sure to hit the ball with the top of your forehead. Hitting the ball with the your head won't hurt if you use your forehead.
  b. keep your eyes open and watch the ball as your head hits it.
  c. keep your mouth closed.
  d. swing your body from the waist to get good power.

NOTE: To head the ball high:
  a. you should bend backward a little at the waist as the ball moves toward you.
  b. you should snap your body forward at the waist as you hit the ball.
  c. your forehead should hit the ball below its center line.

Today's Scores

YOUR GOAL: A score of 2 or more hits

	1	2	3	4	5	6	7	8	9	10	11	12	13	14	15	16	17	18	19	20
NUMBER OF HITS																				

How To Watch Your Score Improve

1. Write down your score for today. The first day you do this drill, write your score by **DAY 1**, Write you score for the second day by **DAY 2**, and so on.

2. Did you meet your goal?

NO!

Erase **"Today's Scores"** and do this drill again the next time you **PRACTICE SOCCER BY YOURSELF.**

YES!

WELL DONE! The next time you **PRACTICE SOCCER BY YOURSELF** you can move up to the drill on the next page.

Also cut off the number on the top of this page. Then turn to the **PROGRESS CHART** at the end of the book.

DAY	SCORE	DAY	SCORE	DAY	SCORE
1		11		21	
2		12		22	
3		13		23	
4		14		24	
5		15		25	
6		16		26	
7		17		27	
8		18		28	
9		19		29	
10		20		30	

NOTES:

TWO-TOUCH REBOUNDING
AT LEFT/RIGHT SMALL TARGETS

What You Need To Do This Drill
- A small area of flat ground with a wall at one end
- A soccer ball
- Two markers (sticks, cans, rags, etc.)
- This page, a pencil and an eraser

How to Set Up For This Drill
A. Draw two targets on the wall. The left target is one large step wide and goes from the ground to as high as you can reach. The right target is one large step wide and goes from the ground to as high as you can reach.

B. Set up the markers 5 large steps from the wall and 8 large steps apart.

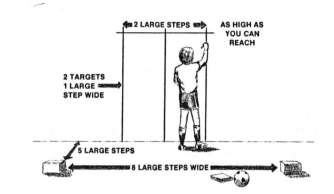

How To Do This Drill
1. Place the ball on the ground in front of the target and further from the wall than the markers.
2. Kick the ball at the right hand target on the wall.
3. When the ball bounces off the right hand target, stop the ball with your leg or foot or body. Don't go closer to the wall than the markers.
4. Kick the ball at the left target. Don't go closer to the wall than the markers.
5. Every time the ball bounces off the left target, stop the ball with your leg or foot or body. Then kick the ball at the right hand target. When the ball bounces off the right hand target, stop the ball with your leg or foot or body. Then kick the ball at the left target. Kick at one target, then the other: right hand target—stop the ball—left hand target—stop the ball—right hand target—.
6. Count the number of times in a row you hit the target. This is your score.
7. When you miss the target or don't stop the ball correctly: stop the drill; write down your score in **"Today's Scores."** Then start again at **step 1.**
8. Do this drill for 5 minutes.

NOTE: Look at the target, then look down at the ball as you kick it.

Today's Scores

YOUR GOAL: A score of 6 or more hits

	1	2	3	4	5	6	7	8	9	10	11	12	13	14	15	16	17	18	19	20
NUMBER OF HITS																				

How To Watch Your Score Improve

1. Write down your score for today. The first day you do this drill, write your score by **DAY 1**, Write you score for the second day by **DAY 2**, and so on.

2. Did you meet your goal?

NO!

Erase **"Today's Scores"** and do this drill again the next time you **PRACTICE SOCCER BY YOURSELF.**

YES!

WELL DONE! The next time you **PRACTICE SOCCER BY YOURSELF** you can move up to the drill on the next page.

Also cut off the number on the top of this page. Then turn to the **PROGRESS CHART** at the end of the book.

DAY	SCORE	DAY	SCORE	DAY	SCORE
1		11		21	
2		12		22	
3		13		23	
4		14		24	
5		15		25	
6		16		26	
7		17		27	
8		18		28	
9		19		29	
10		20		30	

NOTES:

WEAK SIDE STOP, TWO-TOUCH REBOUNDING AT LEFT/RIGHT SMALL TARGETS

What You Need To Do This Drill

- A small area of flat ground with a wall at one end
- A soccer ball
- Two markers (sticks, cans, rags, etc.)
- A piece of chalk
- This page, a pencil and an eraser

How to Set Up For This Drill

A. Draw two targets on the wall. The left target is one large step wide and goes from the ground to as high as you can reach. The right target is one large step wide and goes from the ground to as high as you can reach.

B. Set up the markers 5 large steps from the wall and 8 large steps apart.

How To Do This Drill

1. Place the ball on the ground in front of the target and further from the wall than the markers.

2. Kick the ball at the right hand target on the wall.

3. When the ball bounces off the right hand target, stop the ball with your weaker leg or foot. Don't go closer to the wall than the markers.

4. Kick the ball at the left target. Don't go closer to the wall than the markers.

5. Every time the ball bounces off the left target, stop the ball with your weaker leg or foot. Then kick the ball at the right hand target. When the ball bounces off the right hand target, stop the ball with your weaker leg or foot. Then kick the ball at the left target. Kick at one target, then the other: right hand target—stop the ball—left hand target—stop the ball—right hand target—.

6. Count the number of times in a row you hit the target. This is your score.

7. When you miss the target or don't stop the ball correctly: stop the drill; write down your score in **"Today's Scores."** Then start again at **step 1.**

8. Do this drill for 5 minutes.

NOTE: Look at the target, then look down at the ball as you kick it.

NOTE: Kick the ball with the inside of your foot. This type of kick will help you kick the ball where you want it to go.

NOTE: Relax your foot or leg as the ball hits it. This will help to keep the ball near you so you can kick it quickly.

NOTE: To stop the ball you can use the inside, outside, top, or bottom of your foot, or you can use your shins, thighs, stomach, chest or head.

Today's Scores

YOUR GOAL: A score of 6 or more hits

	1	2	3	4	5	6	7	8	9	10	11	12	13	14	15	16	17	18	19	20
NUMBER OF HITS																				

How To Watch Your Score Improve

1. Write down your score for today. The first day you do this drill, write your score by **DAY 1**, Write you score for the second day by **DAY 2**, and so on.

2. Did you meet your goal?

NO!

Erase **"Today's Scores"** and do this drill again the next time you **PRACTICE SOCCER BY YOURSELF.**

YES!

WELL DONE! The next time you **PRACTICE SOCCER BY YOURSELF** you can move up to the drill on the next page.

Also cut off the number on the top of this page. Then turn to the **PROGRESS CHART** at the end of the book.

DAY	SCORE	DAY	SCORE	DAY	SCORE
1		11		21	
2		12		22	
3		13		23	
4		14		24	
5		15		25	
6		16		26	
7		17		27	
8		18		28	
9		19		29	
10		20		30	

NOTES:

ONE-TOUCH REBOUNDING
AT LEFT/RIGHT SMALL TARGETS

What You Need To Do This Drill

- A small area of flat ground with a wall at one end
- A soccer ball
- Two markers (sticks, cans, rags, etc.)
- A piece of chalk
- This page, a pencil and an eraser

How to Set Up For This Drill

A. Draw two targets on the wall. The left target is one large step wide and goes from the ground to as high as you can reach. The right target is one large step wide and goes from the ground to as high as you can reach.

B. Set up the markers 5 large steps from the wall and 8 large steps apart.

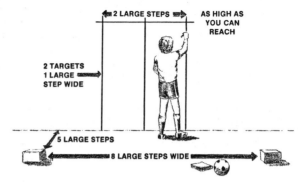

How To Do This Drill

1. Place the ball on the ground in front of the target and further from the wall than the markers.

2. Kick the ball at the right hand target on the wall.

3. When the ball bounces off the right hand target, kick the ball at the left target. Don't go closer to the wall than the markers and DON'T STOP THE BALL BEFORE YOU KICK IT.

4. Every time the ball bounces off the left target, kick the ball at the right hand target. When the ball bounces off the right hand target, kick the ball at the left target. Kick at one target, then the other: right hand target—left hand target—right hand target—.

6. Count the number of times in a row you hit the target. This is your score.

7. When you miss the target: stop the drill; write down your score in **"Today's Scores."** Then start again at **step 1.**

8. Do this drill for 5 minutes.

NOTE: Look at the target, then look down at the ball as you kick it.

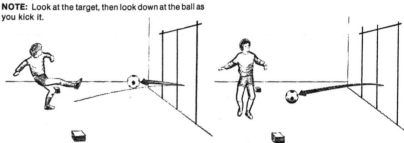

NOTE: Kick the ball with the inside of your foot. This type of kick will help you kick the ball where you want it to go.

Today's Scores

YOUR GOAL: A score of 6 or more hits

	1	2	3	4	5	6	7	8	9	10	11	12	13	14	15	16	17	18	19	20
NUMBER OF HITS																				

How To Watch Your Score Improve

1. Write down your score for today. The first day you do this drill, write your score by **DAY 1**, Write you score for the second day by **DAY 2**, and so on.

2. Did you meet your goal?

NO!

Erase **"Today's Scores"** and do this drill again the next time you **PRACTICE SOCCER BY YOURSELF.**

YES!

WELL DONE! The next time you **PRACTICE SOCCER BY YOURSELF** you can move up to the drill on the next page.

Also cut off the number on the top of this page. Then turn to the **PROGRESS CHART** at the end of the book.

DAY	SCORE		DAY	SCORE		DAY	SCORE
1			11			21	
2			12			22	
3			13			23	
4			14			24	
5			15			25	
6			16			26	
7			17			27	
8			18			28	
9			19			29	
10			20			30	

NOTES:

WEAK FOOT KICK, ONE-TOUCH REBOUNDING AT LEFT/RIGHT SMALL TARGETS

What You Need To Do This Drill

- A small area of flat ground with a wall at one end
- A soccer ball
- Two markers (sticks, cans, rags, etc.)
- A piece of chalk
- This page, a pencil and an eraser

How to Set Up For This Drill

A. Draw two targets on the wall. The left target is one large step wide and goes from the ground to as high as you can reach. The right target is one large step wide and goes from the ground to as high as you can reach.

B. Set up the markers 5 large steps from the wall and 8 large steps apart.

How To Do This Drill

1. Place the ball on the ground in front of the target and further from the wall than the markers.

2. Kick the ball at the right hand target on the wall. Use your weaker foot.

3. When the ball bounces off the right hand target, kick the ball at the left garget. Use your weaker foot. Don't go closer to the wall than the markers and DON'T STOP THE BALL BEFORE YOU KICK IT.

4. Every time the ball bounces off the left target, kick the ball at the right hand target with your weaker foot. When the ball bounces off the right hand target, kick the ball at the left target with your weaker foot. Kick at one target, then the other: right hand target—left hand target—right hand target—.

5. Count the number of times in a row you hit the target. This is your score.

6. When you miss the target or don't stop the ball correctly: stop the drill; write down your score in **"Today's Scores."** Then start again at **step 1.**

7. Do this drill for 5 minutes.

NOTE: Look at the target, then look down at the ball as you kick it.

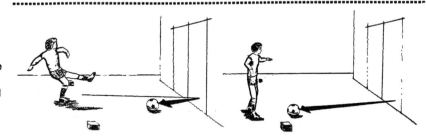

Today's Scores

YOUR GOAL: A score of 5 or more hits

	1	2	3	4	5	6	7	8	9	10	11	12	13	14	15	16	17	18	19	20
NUMBER OF HITS																				

How To Watch Your Score Improve

1. Write down your score for today. The first day you do this drill, write your score by **DAY 1**, Write you score for the second day by **DAY 2**, and so on.

2. Did you meet your goal?

NO!

Erase **"Today's Scores"** and do this drill again the next time you **PRACTICE SOCCER BY YOURSELF.**

YES!

WELL DONE! The next time you **PRACTICE SOCCER BY YOURSELF** you can move up to the drill on the next page.

Also cut off the number on the top of this page. Then turn to the **PROGRESS CHART** at the end of the book.

DAY	SCORE	DAY	SCORE	DAY	SCORE
1		11		21	
2		12		22	
3		13		23	
4		14		24	
5		15		25	
6		16		26	
7		17		27	
8		18		28	
9		19		29	
10		20		30	

NOTES:

TWO-TOUCH REBOUNDING AT HIGH/LOW SMALL TARGETS

What You Need To Do This Drill

- A small area of flat ground with a wall at one end
- A soccer ball
- Two markers (sticks, cans, rags, etc.)
- A piece of chalk
- This page, a pencil and an eraser

How to Set Up For This Drill

A. Draw two targets on the wall. The high target is 2 large steps wide and goes from your waist to as high as you can reach. The low target is two large steps wide and goes from the ground to your waist.

B. Set up the markers 5 large steps from the wall and 8 large steps apart.

How To Do This Drill

1. Place the ball on the ground in front of the target and further from the wall than the markers.

2. Kick the ball at the bottom target on the wall.

3. When the ball bounces off the bottom target, stop the ball with your leg or foot or body. Don't go closer to the wall than the markers.

4. Kick the ball at the top target. Don't go closer to the wall than the markers.

5. Every time the ball bounces off the top target, stop the ball with your leg or foot or body. Then kick the ball at the bottom target. When the ball bounces off the bottom target, stop the ball with your leg or foot or body. Then kick the ball at the top target. Kick at one target, then the other: top target—stop the ball—bottom target—stop the ball—top target—.

6. Count the number of times in a row you hit the target. This is your score.

7. When you miss the correct target: stop the drill; write down your score in **"Today's Scores."** Then start again at **step 1.**

8. Do this drill for 5 minutes.

NOTE: Look at the target, then look down at the ball as you kick it.

Today's Scores

YOUR GOAL: A score of 4 or more hits

	1	2	3	4	5	6	7	8	9	10	11	12	13	14	15	16	17	18	19	20
NUMBER OF HITS																				

How To Watch Your Score Improve

1. Write down your score for today. The first day you do this drill, write your score by **DAY 1**, Write you score for the second day by **DAY 2**, and so on.

2. Did you meet your goal?

NO!

Erase **"Today's Scores"** and do this drill again the next time you **PRACTICE SOCCER BY YOURSELF.**

YES!

WELL DONE! The next time you **PRACTICE SOCCER BY YOURSELF** you can move up to the drill on the next page.

Also cut off the number on the top of this page. Then turn to the **PROGRESS CHART** at the end of the book.

DAY	SCORE		DAY	SCORE		DAY	SCORE
1			11			21	
2			12			22	
3			13			23	
4			14			24	
5			15			25	
6			16			26	
7			17			27	
8			18			28	
9			19			29	
10			20			30	

NOTES:

WEAK SIDE STOP, TWO-TOUCH REBOUNDING AT HIGH/LOW SMALL TARGETS

What You Need To Do This Drill

- A small area of flat ground with a wall at one end
- A soccer ball
- Two markers (sticks, cans, rags, etc.)
- A piece of chalk
- This page, a pencil and an eraser

How to Set Up For This Drill

A. Draw two targets on the wall. The high target is 2 large steps wide and goes from your waist to as high as you can reach. The low target is two large steps wide and goes from the ground to your waist.

B. Set up the markers 5 large steps from the wall and 8 large steps apart.

How To Do This Drill

1. Place the ball on the ground in front of the target and further from the wall than the markers.

2. Kick the ball at the bottom target on the wall.

3. When the ball bounces off the bottom target, stop the ball with your weaker leg or foot. Don't go closer to the wall than the markers.

4. Kick the ball at the top target. Don't go closer to the wall than the markers.

5. Every time the ball bounces off the top target, stop the ball with your weaker leg or foot. Then kick the ball at the bottom target. When the ball bounces off the bottom target, stop the ball with your weaker leg or foot. Then kick the ball at the top target. Kick at one target, then the other: top target—stop the ball—bottom target—stop the ball—top target—.

6. Count the number of times in a row you hit the target. This is your score.

7. When you miss the correct target or don't stop the ball correctly: stop the drill; write down your score in **"Today's Scores."** Then start again at **step 1.**

8. Do this drill for 5 minutes.

NOTE: To kick the ball low, bend your body forward over the ball.

NOTE: To kick the ball low, kick it at or above its center point.

NOTE: To kick the ball high, kick it below its center point.

NOTE: To kick the ball high, bend your body backward away from the ball.

Today's Scores

YOUR GOAL: A score of 4 or more hits

	1	2	3	4	5	6	7	8	9	10	11	12	13	14	15	16	17	18	19	20
NUMBER OF HITS																				

How To Watch Your Score Improve

1. Write down your score for today. The first day you do this drill, write your score by **DAY 1**, Write you score for the second day by **DAY 2**, and so on.

2. Did you meet your goal?

NO!

Erase **"Today's Scores"** and do this drill again the next time you **PRACTICE SOCCER BY YOURSELF.**

YES!

WELL DONE! The next time you **PRACTICE SOCCER BY YOURSELF** you can move up to the drill on the next page.

Also cut off the number on the top of this page. Then turn to the **PROGRESS CHART** at the end of the book.

DAY	SCORE
1	
2	
3	
4	
5	
6	
7	
8	
9	
10	

DAY	SCORE
11	
12	
13	
14	
15	
16	
17	
18	
19	
20	

DAY	SCORE
21	
22	
23	
24	
25	
26	
27	
28	
29	
30	

NOTES:

ONE-TOUCH REBOUNDING AT HIGH/LOW SMALL TARGETS

What You Need To Do This Drill
- A small area of flat ground with a wall at one end
- A soccer ball
- Two markers (sticks, cans, rags, etc.)
- A piece of chalk
- This page, a pencil and an eraser

How to Set Up For This Drill
A. Draw two targets on the wall. The high target is 2 large steps wide and goes from your waist to as high as you can reach. The low target is two large steps wide and goes from the ground to your waist.

B. Set up the markers 5 large steps from the wall and 8 large steps apart.

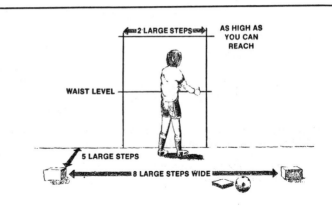

How To Do This Drill
1. Place the ball on the ground in front of the target and further from the wall than the markers.

2. Kick the ball at the bottom target on the wall.

3. When the ball bounces off the bottom target, kick the ball at the top target. Don't go closer to the wall than the markers and DON'T STOP THE BALL BEFORE YOU KICK IT.

4. Every time the ball bounces off the top target, kick the ball at the bottom target. When the ball bounces off the bottom target, kick the ball at the top target. Kick at one target, then the other: top target—bottom target—top target—.

6. Count the number of times in a row you hit the target. This is your score.

7. When you miss the correct target: stop the drill; write down your score in **"Today's Scores."** Then start again at **step 1.**

8. Do this drill for 5 minutes.

Today's Scores

YOUR GOAL: A score of 4 or more hits

	1	2	3	4	5	6	7	8	9	10	11	12	13	14	15	16	17	18	19	20
NUMBER OF HITS																				

How To Watch Your Score Improve

1. Write down your score for today. The first day you do this drill, write your score by **DAY 1**, Write you score for the second day by **DAY 2**, and so on.

2. Did you meet your goal?

NO!

Erase **"Today's Scores"** and do this drill again the next time you **PRACTICE SOCCER BY YOURSELF.**

YES!

WELL DONE! The next time you **PRACTICE SOCCER BY YOURSELF** you can move up to the drill on the next page.

Also cut off the number on the top of this page. Then turn to the **PROGRESS CHART** at the end of the book.

DAY	SCORE
1	
2	
3	
4	
5	
6	
7	
8	
9	
10	

DAY	SCORE
11	
12	
13	
14	
15	
16	
17	
18	
19	
20	

DAY	SCORE
21	
22	
23	
24	
25	
26	
27	
28	
29	
30	

NOTES:

WEAK FOOT KICK,
ONE-TOUCH REBOUNDING AT HIGH/LOW SMALL TARGETS

What You Need To Do This Drill

- A small area of flat ground with a wall at one end
- A soccer ball
- Two markers (sticks, cans, rags, etc.)
- A piece of chalk
- This page, a pencil and an eraser

How to Set Up For This Drill

A. Draw two targets on the wall. The high target is 2 large steps wide and goes from your waist to as high as you can reach. The low target is two large steps wide and goes from the ground to your waist.

B. Set up the markers 5 large steps from the wall and 8 large steps apart.

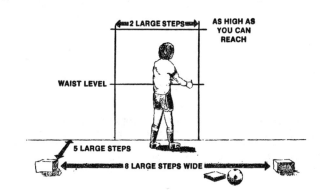

How To Do This Drill

1. Place the ball on the ground in front of the target and further from the wall than the markers.

2. Kick the ball at the bottom target on the wall. Use your weaker foot.

3. When the ball bounces off the bottom target, kick the ball at the top target. Use your weaker foot. Don't go closer to the wall than the markers and DON'T STOP THE BALL BEFORE YOU KICK IT.

4. Every time the ball bounces off the top target, kick the ball at the bottom target with your weaker foot. When the ball bounces off the bottom target, kick the ball at the top target with your weaker foot. Kick at one target, then the other: top target—bottom barget—top target—.

5. Count the number of times in a row you hit the correct target. This is your score.

6. When you miss the correct target or don't kick the ball correctly: stop the drill; write down your score in **"Today's Scores."** Then start again at **step 1.**

7. Do this drill for 5 minutes.

Today's Scores

YOUR GOAL: A score of 4 or more hits

	1	2	3	4	5	6	7	8	9	10	11	12	13	14	15	16	17	18	19	20
NUMBER OF HITS																				

How To Watch Your Score Improve

1. Write down your score for today. The first day you do this drill, write your score by **DAY 1**, Write you score for the second day by **DAY 2**, and so on.

2. Did you meet your goal?

NO!

Erase **"Today's Scores"** and do this drill again the next time you **PRACTICE SOCCER BY YOURSELF.**

YES!

WELL DONE! The next time you **PRACTICE SOCCER BY YOURSELF** you can move up to the drill on the next page.

Also cut off the number on the top of this page. Then turn to the **PROGRESS CHART** at the end of the book.

DAY	SCORE
1	
2	
3	
4	
5	
6	
7	
8	
9	
10	

DAY	SCORE
11	
12	
13	
14	
15	
16	
17	
18	
19	
20	

DAY	SCORE
21	
22	
23	
24	
25	
26	
27	
28	
29	
30	

NOTES:

HEAD CLEAR REBOUNDING

What You Need To Do This Drill
- A small area of flat ground with a wall at one end
- A soccer ball
- This page, a pencil and an eraser

How to Set Up For This Drill
A. No set up is needed

How To Do This Drill

1. Stand about three steps out from the wall, holding the ball and facing the wall.

2. Throw the ball high up on the wall.

3. When it bounces off the wall, hit the ball back up on the wall with your forehead. Don't let the ball touch the ground.

4. Every time the ball bounces off the wall, head the ball back up on the wall.

5. Count the number of times in a row you hit the ball up on the wall with your head before the ball drops to the ground. This is your score.

6. When the ball drops to the ground; stop the drill; write down your score in **"Todays Scores."** then start again at **step 1.**

7. Do this drill for 5 minutes.

NOTE: When you hit the ball with your head:
    a. be sure to hit the ball with the top of your forehead. Hitting the ball with the your head won't hurt if you use your forehead.
    b. keep your eyes open and watch the ball as your head hits it.
    c. keep your mouth closed.
    d. swing your body from the waist to get good power.

NOTE: To head the ball high:
    a. you should bend backward a little at the waist as the ball moves toward you.
    b. you should snap your body forward at the waist as you hit the ball.
    c. your forehead should hit the ball below its center line.

Today's Scores

YOUR GOAL: A score of 4 or more hits

	1	2	3	4	5	6	7	8	9	10	11	12	13	14	15	16	17	18	19	20
NUMBER OF HITS																				

How To Watch Your Score Improve

1. Write down your score for today. The first day you do this drill, write your score by **DAY 1**, Write you score for the second day by **DAY 2**, and so on.

2. Did you meet your goal?

NO!

Erase **"Today's Scores"** and do this drill again the next time you **PRACTICE SOCCER BY YOURSELF.**

YES!

WELL DONE! The next time you **PRACTICE SOCCER BY YOURSELF** you can move up to the drill on the next page.

Also cut off the number on the top of this page. Then turn to the **PROGRESS CHART** at the end of the book.

DAY	SCORE	DAY	SCORE	DAY	SCORE
1		11		21	
2		12		22	
3		13		23	
4		14		24	
5		15		25	
6		16		26	
7		17		27	
8		18		28	
9		19		29	
10		20		30	

NOTES:

TWO-TOUCH REBOUNDING AT LEFT/RIGHT LOW TARGETS

What You Need To Do This Drill

- A small area of flat ground with a wall at one end
- A soccer ball
- Two markers (sticks, cans, rags, etc.)
- A piece of chalk
- This page, a pencil and an eraser

How to Set Up For This Drill

A. Draw two targets on the wall. The left target is one large step wide and goes from the ground to your waist. The right target is one large step wide and goes from the ground to your waist.

B. Set up the markers 5 large steps from the wall and 8 large steps apart.

How To Do This Drill

1. Place the ball on the ground in front of the target and further from the wall than the markers.

2. Kick the ball at the right hand target on the wall.

3. When the ball bounces off the right hand target, stop the ball with your leg or foot or body. Don't go closer to the wall than the markers.

4. Kick the ball at the left target. Don't go closer to the wall than the markers.

5. Every time the ball bounces off the left target, stop the ball with your leg or foot or body. Then kick the ball at the right hand target. When the ball bounces off the right hand target, stop the ball with your leg or foot or body. Then kick the ball at the left target. Kick at one target, then the other: right hand target—stop the ball—left hand target—stop the ball—right hand target—.

6. Count the number of times in a row you hit the correct target. This is your score.

7. When you miss the correct target: stop the drill; write down your score in **"Today's Scores."** Then start again at **step 1.**

8. Do this drill for 5 minutes.

NOTE: Look at the target, then look down at the ball as you kick it.

NOTE: To stop the ball you can use the inside, outside, top, or bottom of your foot, or you can use your shins, thighs, stomach, chest or head.

NOTE: Relax your foot or leg as the ball hits it. This will help to keep the ball near you so you can kick it quickly.

NOTE: Kick the ball with your instep. This type of kick is for power and distance.

Today's Scores

YOUR GOAL: A score of 10 or more hits

	1	2	3	4	5	6	7	8	9	10	11	12	13	14	15	16	17	18	19	20
NUMBER OF HITS																				

How To Watch Your Score Improve

1. Write down your score for today. The first day you do this drill, write your score by **DAY 1**, Write you score for the second day by **DAY 2**, and so on.

2. Did you meet your goal?

NO!

Erase **"Today's Scores"** and do this drill again the next time you **PRACTICE SOCCER BY YOURSELF.**

YES!

WELL DONE! The next time you **PRACTICE SOCCER BY YOURSELF** you can move up to the drill on the next page.

Also cut off the number on the top of this page. Then turn to the **PROGRESS CHART** at the end of the book.

DAY	SCORE
1	
2	
3	
4	
5	
6	
7	
8	
9	
10	

DAY	SCORE
11	
12	
13	
14	
15	
16	
17	
18	
19	
20	

DAY	SCORE
21	
22	
23	
24	
25	
26	
27	
28	
29	
30	

NOTES:

WEAK SIDE STOP,
TWO-TOUCH REBOUNDING AT LEFT/RIGHT LOW TARGETS

What You Need To Do This Drill
- A small area of flat ground with a wall at one end
- A soccer ball
- Two markers (sticks, cans, rags, etc.)
- A piece of chalk
- This page, a pencil and an eraser

How to Set Up For This Drill
A. Draw two targets on the wall. The left target is one large step wide and goes from the ground to your waist. The right target is one large step wide and goes from the ground to your waist.

B. Set up the markers 5 large steps from the wall and 8 large steps apart.

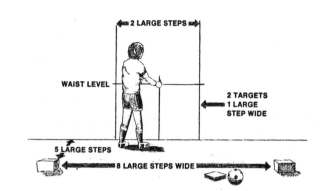

How To Do This Drill
1. Place the ball on the ground in front of the target and further from the wall than the markers.

2. Kick the ball at the right hand target on the wall.

3. When the ball bounces off the right hand target, stop the ball with your weaker leg or foot. Don't go closer to the wall than the markers.

4. Kick the ball at the left target. Don't go closer to the wall than the markers.

5. Every time the ball bounces off the left target, stop the ball with your weaker leg or foot. Then kick the ball at the right hand target. When the ball bounces off the right hand target, stop the ball with your weaker leg or foot. Then kick the ball at the left target. Kick at one target, then the other: right hand target—stop the ball—left hand target—stop the ball—right hand target—.

6. Count the number of times in a row you hit the correct target. This is your score.

7. When you miss the correct target or don't stop the ball correctly: stop the drill; write down your score in **"Today's Scores."** Then start again at **step 1.**

8. Do this drill for 5 minutes.

Today's Scores

YOUR GOAL: A score of 10 or more hits

	1	2	3	4	5	6	7	8	9	10	11	12	13	14	15	16	17	18	19	20
NUMBER OF HITS																				

How To Watch Your Score Improve

1. Write down your score for today. The first day you do this drill, write your score by **DAY 1,** Write you score for the second day by **DAY 2**, and so on.

2. Did you meet your goal?

NO!

Erase **"Today's Scores"** and do this drill again the next time you **PRACTICE SOCCER BY YOURSELF.**

YES!

WELL DONE! The next time you **PRACTICE SOCCER BY YOURSELF** you can move up to the drill on the next page.

Also cut off the number on the top of this page. Then turn to the **PROGRESS CHART** at the end of the book.

DAY	SCORE	DAY	SCORE	DAY	SCORE
1		11		21	
2		12		22	
3		13		23	
4		14		24	
5		15		25	
6		16		26	
7		17		27	
8		18		28	
9		19		29	
10		20		30	

NOTES:

ONE-TOUCH REBOUNDING AT LEFT/RIGHT LOW TARGETS

What You Need To Do This Drill

- A small area of flat ground with a wall at one end
- A soccer ball
- Two markers (sticks, cans, rags, etc.)
- A piece of chalk
- This page, a pencil and an eraser

How to Set Up For This Drill

A. Draw two targets on the wall. The left target is one large step wide and goes from the ground to your waist. The right target is one large step wide and goes from the ground to your waist.

B. Set up the markers 5 large steps from the wall and 8 large steps apart.

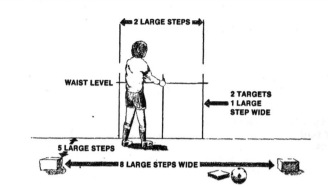

How To Do This Drill

1. Place the ball on the ground in front of the target and further from the wall than the markers.

2. Kick the ball at the bottom right hand target on the wall.

3. When the ball bounces off the right hand target, kick the ball at the left hand target. Don't go closer to the wall than the markers and DON'T STOP THE BALL BEFORE YOU KICK IT.

4. Every time the ball bounces off the left target, kick the ball at the right hand target. When the ball bounces off the right hand target, kick the ball at the left target. Kick at one target, then the other: right hand target—left hand target—right hand target—.

5. Count the number of times in a row you hit the correct target. This is your score.

7. When you miss the correct target: stop the drill; write down your score in **"Today's Scores."** Then start again at **step 1.**

8. Do this drill for 5 minutes.

Today's Scores

YOUR GOAL: A score of 8 or more hits

	1	2	3	4	5	6	7	8	9	10	11	12	13	14	15	16	17	18	19	20
NUMBER OF HITS																				

How To Watch Your Score Improve

1. Write down your score for today. The first day you do this drill, write your score by **DAY 1**, Write you score for the second day by **DAY 2**, and so on.

2. Did you meet your goal?

NO!

Erase **"Today's Scores"** and do this drill again the next time you **PRACTICE SOCCER BY YOURSELF.**

YES!

WELL DONE! The next time you **PRACTICE SOCCER BY YOURSELF** you can move up to the drill on the next page.

Also cut off the number on the top of this page. Then turn to the **PROGRESS CHART** at the end of the book.

DAY	SCORE		DAY	SCORE		DAY	SCORE
1			11			21	
2			12			22	
3			13			23	
4			14			24	
5			15			25	
6			16			26	
7			17			27	
8			18			28	
9			19			29	
10			20			30	

NOTES:

WEAK FOOT KICK,
ONE-TOUCH REBOUNDING AT LEFT/RIGHT LOW TARGETS

What You Need To Do This Drill

- A small area of flat ground with a wall at one end
- A soccer ball
- Two markers (sticks, cans, rags, etc.)
- A piece of chalk
- This page, a pencil and an eraser

How To Set Up For This Drill

A. Draw two targets on the wall. The left target is one large step wide and goes from the ground to your waist. The right target is one large step wide and goes from the ground to your waist.

B. Set up the markers 5 large steps from the wall and 8 large steps apart.

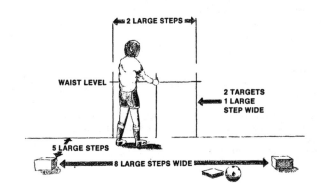

How To Do This Drill

1. Place the ball on the ground in front of the target and further from the wall than the markers.

2. Kick the ball at the right hand target on the wall. Use your weaker foot.

3. When the ball bounces off the right hand target, kick the ball at the left hand target. Don't go closer to the wall than the markers and DON'T STOP THE BALL BEFORE YOU KICK IT.

4. Every time the ball bounces off the left target, kick the ball at the right hand target with your weaker foot. When the ball bounces off the right hand target, kick the ball at the left target with your weaker foot. Kick at one target, then the other: right hand target—left hand target—right hand target—.

5. Count the number of times in a row you hit the correct target. This is your score.

7. When you miss the correct target or don't kick the ball correctly: stop the drill; write down your score in **"Today's Scores."** Then start again at **step 1.**

8. Do this drill for 5 minutes.

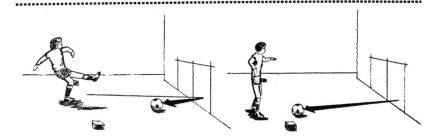

Today's Scores

YOUR GOAL: A score of 6 or more hits

	1	2	3	4	5	6	7	8	9	10	11	12	13	14	15	16	17	18	19	20
NUMBER OF HITS																				

How To Watch Your Score Improve

1. Write down your score for today. The first day you do this drill, write your score by **DAY 1**, Write you score for the second day by **DAY 2**, and so on.

2. Did you meet your goal?

NO!

Erase **"Today's Scores"** and do this drill again the next time you **PRACTICE SOCCER BY YOURSELF.**

YES!

WELL DONE! The next time you **PRACTICE SOCCER BY YOURSELF** you can move up to the drill on the next page.

Also cut off the number on the top of this page. Then turn to the **PROGRESS CHART** at the end of the book.

DAY	SCORE	DAY	SCORE	DAY	SCORE
1		11		21	
2		12		22	
3		13		23	
4		14		24	
5		15		25	
6		16		26	
7		17		27	
8		18		28	
9		19		29	
10		20		30	

NOTES:

HEAD CLEAR REBOUNDING

What You Need To Do This Drill
- A small area of flat ground with a wall at one end
- A soccer ball
- This page, a pencil and an eraser

How to Set Up For This Drill
A. No set up is needed

How To Do This Drill

1. Stand about three steps out from the wall, holding the ball and facing the wall.

2. Throw the ball high up on the wall.

3. When it bounces off the wall, hit the ball back up on the wall with your forehead. Don't let the ball touch the ground.

4. Every time the ball bounces off the wall, head the ball back up on the wall.

5. Count the number of times in a row you hit the ball up on the wall with your head before the ball drops to the ground. This is your score.

6. When the ball drops to the ground; stop the drill; write down your score in **"Todays Scores."** then start again at **step 1.**

7. Do this drill for 5 minutes.

NOTE: When you hit the ball with your head:
   a. be sure to hit the ball with the top of your forehead. Hitting the ball with the your head won't hurt if you use your forehead.
   b. keep your eyes open and watch the ball as your head hits it.
   c. keep your mouth closed.
   d. swing your body from the waist to get good power.

NOTE: To head the ball high:
   a. you should bend backward a little at the waist as the ball moves toward you.
   b. you should snap your body forward at the waist as you hit the ball.
   c. your forehead should hit the ball below its center line.

Today's Scores

YOUR GOAL: A score of 5 or more hits

	1	2	3	4	5	6	7	8	9	10	11	12	13	14	15	16	17	18	19	20
NUMBER OF HITS																				

How To Watch Your Score Improve

1. Write down your score for today. The first day you do this drill, write your score by **DAY 1**, Write you score for the second day by **DAY 2**, and so on.

2. Did you meet your goal?

NO!

Erase **"Today's Scores"** and do this drill again the next time you **PRACTICE SOCCER BY YOURSELF.**

YES!

WELL DONE! The next time you **PRACTICE SOCCER BY YOURSELF** you can move up to the drill on the next page.

Also cut off the number on the top of this page. Then turn to the **PROGRESS CHART** at the end of the book.

DAY	SCORE	DAY	SCORE	DAY	SCORE
1		11		21	
2		12		22	
3		13		23	
4		14		24	
5		15		25	
6		16		26	
7		17		27	
8		18		28	
9		19		29	
10		20		30	

NOTES:

TWO-TOUCH REBOUNDING AT LEFT/RIGHT HIGH TARGETS

What You Need To Do This Drill

- A small area of flat ground with a wall at one end
- A soccer ball
- Two markers (sticks, cans, rags, etc.)
- A piece of chalk
- This page, a pencil and an eraser

How to Set Up For This Drill

A. Draw two targets on the wall. The left target is one large step wide and goes from your waist to as high as you can reach. The right target is one large stewp wide and goes from your waist to as high as you can reach.

B. Set up the markers 5 large steps from the wall and 8 large steps apart.

AS HIGH AS YOU CAN REACH

2 TARGETS
1 LARGE STEP WIDE

WAIST LEVEL

5 LARGE STEPS

8 LARGE STEPS WIDE

How To Do This Drill

1. Place the ball on the ground in front of the target and further from the wall than the markers.

2. Kick the ball at the right hand target on the wall.

3. When the ball bounces off the right hand target, stop the ball with your leg or foot or body. Don't go closer to the wall than the markers.

4. Kick the ball at the left target. Don't go closer to the wall than the markers.

5. Every time the ball bounces off the left target, stop the ball with your leg or foot or body. Then kick the ball at the right hand target. When the ball bounces off the right hand target, stop the ball with your leg or foot or body. Then kick the ball at the left target. Kick at one target, then the other: right hand target—stop the ball—left hand target—stop the ball—right hand target—.

6. Count the number of times in a row you hit the correct target. This is your score.

7. When you miss the correct target: stop the drill; write down your score in **"Today's Scores."** Then start again at **step 1.**

8. Do this drill for 5 minutes.

NOTE: Look at the target, then look down at the ball as you kick it.

NOTE: To stop the ball you can use the inside, outside, top, or bottom of your foot, or you can use your shins, thighs, stomach, chest or head.

NOTE: Relax your foot or leg as the ball hits it. This will help to keep the ball near you so you can kick it quickly.

NOTE: Kick the ball with your instep. This type of kick is for power and distance.

Today's Scores

YOUR GOAL: A score of 4 or more hits

	1	2	3	4	5	6	7	8	9	10	11	12	13	14	15	16	17	18	19	20
NUMBER OF HITS																				

How To Watch Your Score Improve

1. Write down your score for today. The first day you do this drill, write your score by **DAY 1**, Write you score for the second day by **DAY 2**, and so on.

2. Did you meet your goal?

NO!

Erase **"Today's Scores"** and do this drill again the next time you **PRACTICE SOCCER BY YOURSELF.**

YES!

WELL DONE! The next time you **PRACTICE SOCCER BY YOURSELF** you can move up to the drill on the next page.

Also cut off the number on the top of this page. Then turn to the **PROGRESS CHART** at the end of the book.

DAY	SCORE	DAY	SCORE	DAY	SCORE
1		11		21	
2		12		22	
3		13		23	
4		14		24	
5		15		25	
6		16		26	
7		17		27	
8		18		28	
9		19		29	
10		20		30	

NOTES:

SUGGESTION FORM

Please use this form if you wish to suggest a drill to be included in the next edition of **PRACTICE SOCCER BY YOURSELF**. If you are the first to suggest the drill and it is included in the next edition you will receive a $100.00 prize and your name will appear together with the drill.

CAUTION: Only skill, technique or tactics drills **that can be practiced alone** will be considered. Fitness drills that do not improve skill, technique or tactics will **not** be considered.

YOUR NAME: _____

ADDRESS: _____

CITY: _____ STATE: _____ ZIP: _____

☐ Check here if you want your club's name included with yours in the book.

YOUR CLUB'S NAME: _____

PLEASE TYPE OR PRINT CLEARLY

Objective Of The Drill

Use the space aside to discuss the skill, technique, or tactic to be learned by players who practice this drill.

Objectives. . .

What You Need To Do This Drill

List all of the equipment and facilities needed to do this drill

What you need. . .

How To Set Up For This Drill

Give a step-by-step procedure that the player must follow to prepare the facilities and equipment so that he or she can perform the drill correctly. Include illustrations as needed to show layout.

How to set up. . .

How To Do This Drill

Give the step-by-step procedure that the player must follow to do this drill. Include illustrations to show important or difficult steps, or to show proper technique.

How to do. . .

PLEASE CONTINUE ON THE OTHER SIDE

SUGGESTION FORM (Continued)

How to do (continued)...

How To Watch Your Skills Improve

Give a step-by-step procedure that the player can use for scoring his or her performance on the drill.

How to watch...

Other Considerations

Include any other factors that you think should be considered in evaluating this drill for inclusion in **PRACTICE SOCCER BY YOURSELF.**

MAILING INSTRUCTIONS

Only those drills submitted by Registered or Certified Mail with a clear return name and address on the envelope will be considered.

You will be notified if your drill is to be included in the next edition of:
PRACTICE SOCCER BY YOURSELF.

No suggestion forms will be returned.

Please mail your suggestions to:

PRACTICE SOCCER BY YOURSELF
c/o H.D. Jones
Florance Gordon and Brown
815 Mutual Bldg.
Richmond, VA 23219

WELL DONE!

Now that you have completed another drill,
be sure to color that box with the
drill number inside of it.

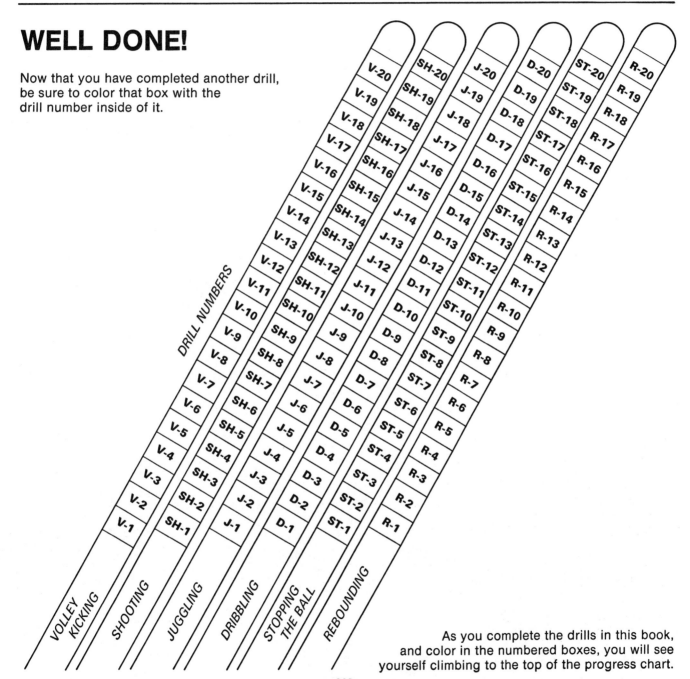

DRILL NUMBERS

VOLLEY KICKING — V-1 through V-20
SHOOTING — SH-1 through SH-20
JUGGLING — J-1 through J-20
DRIBBLING — D-1 through D-20
STOPPING THE BALL — ST-1 through ST-20
REBOUNDING — R-1 through R-20

As you complete the drills in this book,
and color in the numbered boxes, you will see
yourself climbing to the top of the progress chart.